C000245771

# Bridges from the Word
## to the World

# Bridges *from the* Word

## to the World

Ian Coffey with Kim Bush

Text copyright © Ian Coffey and Kim Bush 2007
The authors assert the moral right
to be identified as the authors of this work

**Published by**
**The Bible Reading Fellowship**
First Floor, Elsfield Hall
15–17 Elsfield Way, Oxford OX2 8FG
Website: www.brf.org.uk

ISBN-10: 1 84101 385 4
ISBN-13: 978 1 84101 385 5
First published 2007
10 9 8 7 6 5 4 3 2 1 0
All rights reserved

**Acknowledgments**
Unless otherwise stated, scripture quotations are taken from the Holy Bible, New
International Version, copyright © 1973, 1978, 1984 by International Bible Society,
are used by permission of Hodder & Stoughton, a division of Hodder Headline Ltd.
All rights reserved. 'NIV' is a registered trademark of International Bible Society. UK
trademark number 1448790.

Scripture quotations from THE MESSAGE. Copyright © by Eugene H. Peterson 1993,
1994, 1995. Used by permission of NavPress Publishing.

Scripture quotations marked (Living Water) are taken from the Holy Bible, New Living
Translation, copyright © 1996. Used by permission of Tyndale House Publishers Inc.,
Wheaton, Illinois 60189. All rights reserved.

Scriptures quoted from the Good News Bible published by The Bible Societies/
HarperCollins Publishers Ltd, UK © American Bible Society 1966, 1971, 1976, 1992,
used with permission.

Extracts from the Authorized Version of the Bible (The King James Bible), the rights in
which are vested in the Crown, are reproduced by permission of the Crown's patentee,
Cambridge University Press.

'One Solitary Life' adapted from a sermon by Dr James Allen Francis in *The Real Jesus
and Other Sermons* (Judson Press, 1926)

A catalogue record for this book is available from the British Library

Printed in Singapore by Craft Print International Ltd

# Contents

## The Way We Live

## Points of View

## In Training

## The Armour of God

## Prayer and Praise

## Transformations

## Family Matters

## Hearing from God

# Introduction

Bridges span—it is what they are made to do. With bridges, rivers, valleys, roadways, even stretches of the sea are crossed with ease, and journeys that used to take hours are reduced to seconds.

We chose the title *Bridges from the Word to the World* for this book because it is designed to span some gaps. For example, how can we connect the everyday world with the teaching of the Bible? How can we listen to the news and link what we hear to a living faith? What does it mean (to borrow John Stott's phrase) to 'think Christianly' about the sights and sounds that surround us every day?

The response to the two previous books in the series—*Windows* and *Doorways*—suggested that a third volume was called for, so here it is.

For ten years, Ian wrote a weekly column for the regional newspaper *The Western Morning News*. His brief as a Christian leader (then living in southwest England) was to offer a religious perspective on the news. *The Coffey Column* became widely read and prompted letters from a wide variety of people, including many who claimed to have no faith. Kim, who had a longstanding interest and involvement in books, began to read and group the weekly columns into topics, adding her own reflections from the Bible on the theme in question.

The result is a collection of readings that seeks to do what bridges are made to do—span.

# Times...

# In the days of your youth

**Make the most of every opportunity.**

COLOSSIANS 4:5

It is said of Mark Twain that, at the age of 18, he considered his father a complete idiot. By the time he reached 21, he was amazed at how much the old man had learnt in three years.

Those turbulent, growing years are often a vital time for change. Opinions are formed, attitudes are shaped and directions for life are set.

Recently, I spent a day with a group of British students who were using a gap year to work in a Third World country. The purpose of their time abroad was not sightseeing or lazing on a beach in the sun. These British students had chosen to work with a development team based in a large slum in an Asian city. They were teaching in a makeshift school, running a crèche, assisting in developing cottage industries and helping to build a safe house for children who would otherwise live rough on the streets.

They earned no wage for their efforts. On the contrary, they had had to raise money to cover their fares and living costs from friends and family here at home. I asked what they had gained from the learning experience so far. 'Getting a new set of values,' said one. 'Realizing how much you get back when you give,' said another. 'The sense of belonging in a team,' said a third.

It wasn't all plain sailing for them. Homesickness, adjusting to the inevitable culture shock and learning some hard truths through living in close proximity to others were just a few of the tough lessons they had. But none regretted the decision to spend time abroad: they recognized that the experience would live with them for years to come.

You couldn't meet a livelier crowd, full of noise and laughter. In a few years they will be bankers, teachers, engineers and nurses, with a growing family and a mortgage. But for now, some vital learning years are being invested in building character and responsibility. They will never be the same again. At least, I sincerely hope not.

A few days before, I had preached about the parable of the good Samaritan and stressed how loving our neighbour meant looking beyond the colour of people's skin and their social status. Jesus concluded the famous parable with the words, 'Go and do likewise' (Luke 10:37).

It was both refreshing and humbling to spend a day with a bunch of students doing exactly that.

## For further reading

ECCLESIASTES 11:7—12:8

There are some opportunities that never come again. Certainly, taking a gap year to go away and do something worthwhile is easier before the additional considerations of family, career and mortgage begin to dominate our lives. While we are young, we should live life to the full, at the same time remembering that God sees all that we do (11:9).

Old age does bring 'days of trouble' for many (12:1), as our bodies —and sometimes our minds—wear out. But all is not doom and gloom: 'However many years people may live, let them enjoy them all' (11:8). The wisdom of age may compensate for the loss of the vigour of youth, and 'Jesus Christ is the same yesterday and today and forever' (Hebrews 13:8). Every day brings new opportunities to please him and demonstrate our devotion to him. If we trust him, we need not hesitate to take the risk of serving him in ways we haven't done before, and we no longer have to say with the writer of Ecclesiastes that 'everything is meaningless' (12:8) because when Jesus returns we will see that 'death has been swallowed up in victory' (1 Corinthians 15:54).

## Prayer

*Ask God if he is calling you to a new way of serving him, or if he is affirming you in how you are living for him right now. Thank him for the opportunities he has given you in the past and for the ones yet to come.*

# For such a time as this

*Written in October 2002*

'Who knows but that you have come to royal position for such a time as this?'
ESTHER 4:14

One of my most vivid childhood memories is of an event that occurred 40 years ago this week.

It was the height of the Cuban missile crisis, a time regarded by many as the closest the world has ever come to nuclear war. The nations held their breath for several days in late October 1962, as a tense stand-off between the USA and the Soviet Union was played out. President Kennedy delivered a stark ultimatum to Khruschev with a clear 'or else...' attached. My childhood memory is of standing in the play-ground at school when a friend remarked casually, 'My mum said the world might end today.'

I've been interested to read various recollections that have appeared to mark the 40th anniversary, including some declassified material that reveals how close we came to war. But one piece of information has intrigued me above all else. In the aftermath of the crisis, when relations between the superpowers were still tense, a US destroyer identified a Soviet submarine off the coast of Cuba. The destroyer attacked, but her captain and crew didn't know that the submarine was carrying nuclear torpedoes, one of which was immediately readied for use.

Under the Soviet rules of engagement, three officers were required to be in agreement before a nuclear strike could be launched. On this occasion, two of the crew on the submarine voted 'yes' but one voted 'no'—and because of the rules, the 'no' vote carried the day.

Last week, the full story emerged at an international conference in Havana, when a senior Soviet naval officer confirmed that this incident —an even nearer miss than the Cuban missile crisis—had occurred. As one US security expert put it in eloquent terms, 'A guy named Arkhipov saved the world.'

Reading the report led me to two important observations. First, never underestimate the power of an individual. We sometimes fall into the trap of thinking that one person can't make a difference to anything, but he or she can. One voice—or one vote—matters.

Second, and I admit this is an unashamedly Christian viewpoint, the final whistle is not in the hands of those who hold power in Washington, Moscow or Baghdad. The world won't end with a bang or a whimper, but with a curtain call.

Khruschev and Kennedy have played their roles and died, but the script moves on to an ending that has already been written.

## For further reading

Esther 7:1–10

Just one man: 'A guy named Arkhipov saved the world.' When he got up that morning, Arkhipov probably didn't foresee a day quite like that. He was in the right place at the right time and he acted with the courage of his convictions.

Esther was just one woman, the only hope—and a small one at that, humanly speaking—for her fellow Jews to escape massacre. She could have kept quiet, refused to take a risk, hoping that she at least would be spared. But she took Mordecai's words and her responsibility seriously and planned her strategy thoughtfully and prayerfully (4:16).

Life is uncertain: we cannot always predict the impact of the actions we take, and perhaps we shouldn't even try. Perhaps we should simply and humbly try to do what is right and leave the outcome to God. Remember that today may be the day when you are in the right place at the right time to make a difference to one other person, or even to the whole world.

## Prayer

*Pray to God for world leaders who hold awesome power for good or evil over the people of their countries. Ask him to give them wisdom to make hard decisions and the humility to know that the power they wield is held in trust and that they are accountable to him for how they use it.*

# In time of war

*Written in March 2003, at the height of the crisis over Iraq*

There is a time for everything... a time for war and a time for peace.

ECCLESIASTES 3:1, 8

Three incidents involving a British leader, an American president and a French president shape our thoughts and prayers in these difficult times. Each story comes from a different page of history.

Sir Francis Drake remains one of the south-west of England's honoured sons. His most famous exploit involved a bold attack on Cadiz harbour in 1587, when he destroyed 33 Spanish ships being prepared to invade England. But Queen Elizabeth I stood resolutely opposed to the attack as she was keen to achieve a diplomatic settlement. It was with great reluctance that she gave the order for Drake to sail from Plymouth. Elizabeth then had second thoughts and sent a dispatch halting the attack, but the message failed to arrive, raising suspicions that Drake knew he would be called back, so pressed on with greater haste.

President De Gaulle was not universally popular over his policy towards Algeria in the 1950s. The French Governor-General, Jacques Soustelle, struggled to support his president and complained that all his friends were attacking his stance. De Gaulle's advice was characteristically blunt: 'Change your friends.'

Abraham Lincoln was dining during the bloody days of the Civil War, and the topic of conversation was the rebellious Southerners. Lincoln refused to join others around the table in speaking of the rebels as vermin to be exterminated. He was challenged by a fiery, patriotic lady who rebuked him for speaking kindly about his enemies instead of destroying them. Lincoln replied, 'Madam, do I not destroy my enemies when I make them my friends?'

These three incidents from history remind us of some important truths. First, division of opinion over war is no new thing and it need not prove fatal to future harmony. Second, we are reminded that such divisions do put great strain on friendships. Contrary to De Gaulle's advice, we don't have to change our friends, just our attitude towards them. Third, we should never lose sight of the human dimension of war. Enemies have names, faces and families too.

There is a fourth truth that should fuel our prayers for service personnel, their anxious families and the millions of innocent and oppressed Iraqis. Wars pass, and the response to the challenge of rebuilding a shattered country reveals the measure of commitment of those who believe in the justice of their cause.

## For further reading

PSALM 79

How does it feel to live in a country that has been invaded by another nation's army? What is it like to find that the invulnerability you had relied upon until then has proved insufficient protection against your enemy? Verses 1–4 and verse 11 of this psalm may call to mind images of war that we have seen on the recent television news, or on older film taken at the time of World War II: pictures of unburied bodies, prisoners of war, ruined cities, survivors amid the rubble of their homes—the places where they had once felt safe.

The reasons for war today are often complicated, stemming from historical grievances, economics, political ideology and flawed human beings. For Israel at the time of the Old Testament, all these things may have played a part, but the psalmist goes back to basics: God's special people have let him down and their deliverance can only come about if they turn back to him (vv. 8–9). Today, in times of fragile peace and terrible suffering, there is only one refuge: God's mercy. We need to depend on him.

## Prayer

*Pray alongside those caught up in war who would say, 'May your mercy come quickly to meet us, for we are in desperate need' (v. 8).*

# The face I deserve

Grey hair is a crown of splendour; it is attained by a righteous life.
PROVERBS 16:31

A couple of days ago, I read a quote that once would have barely mustered my attention. Here it is: 'At fifty, everyone has the face he deserves.' This bold assertion came from the pen of George Orwell, who was pretty bright on other matters, so I suppose is worth listening to on the subject of age!

The words grabbed me forcefully because just last weekend I passed the half-century milestone. Now, courtesy of Orwell, I find myself shaving each morning and wrestling with the question, 'Do I really deserve this face?' Come to think of it, does everyone else deserve it?

I have been treated to a rich selection of witty sayings for weeks now, all on the subject of advancing years. I have shortlisted the best:

- At fifty, your mind makes contracts your body can't keep.
- You now know all the answers but no one asks you the questions.
- You decide to procrastinate but never get around to it.
- You just can't stand people who are intolerant.

The truth is, my needle stuck at 26 and I have never felt any older since. But I suppose reaching 50 marks something about the journey of life, and the jokes keep everyone else happy.

Among all the witty comments, there have been some wise words too—like those from the pen of King David, written in the later years of his life: 'The Lord is my rock, my fortress and my deliverer; my God is my rock, in whom I take refuge... He reached down from on high and took hold of me; he drew me out of deep waters' (2 Samuel 22:2–3, 17).

And then, from Robert Browning (1812–89):

*Grow old along with me!*
*The best is yet to be,*
*The last of life, for which the first was made:*
*Our times are in His hand*
*Who saith, 'A whole I planned,*
*Youth shows but half; trust God: see all, nor be afraid!'*

King David and Browning—two men who lived centuries apart but made the same discovery: that God is good and in his hands life becomes an exciting adventure.

## For further reading

PSALM 121

There is often a tendency to point upwards when talking about God. The answer to the question 'Where does my help come from?' is not 'From the hills' (v. 1) but 'from the Lord, the Maker of heaven and earth' (v. 2). Nowadays we seem to have made an idol of youth. We seek to delay the onset of the appearance of age with more or less drastic measures, from hair dye to plastic surgery. The outward signs of ageing are to be avoided and the inward ones (experience and, we hope, wisdom) are scarcely valued.

Psalm 121 applies to us at whichever stage of life we find ourselves. It is a beautiful picture of a loving God who watches us constantly and protects us (vv. 3–6). If we trust God, we need not fear any change that might take us by surprise; he is watchful and will not be taken off guard. Day or night, in the morning or the sunset of our lives, he will not abandon us. One of the great advantages of being older is that we can look back on how God has helped us in the past and renew our trust in him 'both now and forevermore' (v. 8).

## Prayer

*My help comes from you, Lord. You watch over me and keep me from all harm. I trust you and want to follow you all the days of my life.*

... and Seasons

# A tangle-free new year

No one whose hope is in you will ever be put to shame.
PSALM 25:3

There's embarrassing and there's downright embarrassing, and I guess we have all ended up in both camps at times.

Listening to the radio the other morning, I found comfort in the story of someone else's embarrassment. The lady in question was drying her hair with one of those curling brushes that looks like a small hedgehog with stomach cramp. In the middle of the procedure, her phone rang and she chatted with a friend for a time—actually, quite a long time, because when the call ended she found that the mousse in her hair had set, embedding the brush firmly. She wrestled with it for ages but couldn't work it loose.

Donning a scarf, she shot down the road to a hairdresser's which, mercifully, had few customers. She explained her dilemma to the two stylists, who studied the matted mess in detail. One of them (a woman) said she wouldn't want even to try to get the brush out. The second (a man) said he was game for anything and sat the lady down in a vacant chair.

It took almost an hour of patient cutting, twisting, pulling and prising until, with cheers all round, the man pulled the brush free. But the work had taken its toll on what had once been a fine head of hair. The lady asked her gallant rescuer to restyle her hair at once and try to rescue the situation. Hang the cost, it was the least she could do.

The man looked at her blankly. 'What, me, love? I couldn't restyle your hair if I tried. I'm a window cleaner. I only popped in for a cup of tea!'

As we stand at the junction between one year and the next, it is a good time to stop and think about the big stuff and the tiny details that go to make up the kaleidoscope called life. The parable of the wedged hairbrush has given me a few pointers as well as raising a smile.

First, beware of making quick judgements either about people or situations. As the book of wise sayings puts it, 'It is not good to have zeal without knowledge, nor to be hasty and miss the way' (Proverbs 19:2). Second, be prepared to accept solutions from unlikely sources. Oh, yes, and third, be careful with your hairbrush.

Here's wishing you a happy and tangle-free new year.

## For further reading

EXODUS 3:10—4:17

Some people relish new challenges; others like to stick to what they know and feel capable of doing. Moses was one of the latter. He threw up every obstacle he could think of when God called him to return to Egypt to lead his people out. 'Who am I?' (3:11). 'Who are you?' (v. 13). 'What if the Israelites won't listen to me?' (4:1). 'I'm too tongue-tied to be your spokesman' (v. 10). Finally, when God had answered every objection with his provision, Moses revealed his true feelings: 'O Lord, please send someone else to do it' (v. 13)! He didn't want to be convinced, he wanted to be excused.

Each new year brings fresh challenges, responsibilities and opportunities when we are walking closely with God, and we can be sure that he has been equipping us and will continue to equip us for what he calls us to do. When we step out in faith and obedience, he will not let us down. This doesn't mean that things will always go right or that everything will turn out the way we expect. But if we face slow progress, opposition, thwarted hopes, we should not give up, because we follow the God who does not give up on us.

## Prayer
*Lord, here am I. Send me!*

# Don't forget to write

For the foolishness of God is wiser than human wisdom, and the weakness of God is stronger than human strength.

1 CORINTHIANS 1:25

I wonder if the art of letter writing is dying? According to recent reports, our obsession with e-mail threatens to reduce us to illiteracy. Research shows that most people under the age of 25 have never written a formal letter, but they are dab hands at text messaging and e-mailing, which allow a much more casual style.

Microsoft Hotmail is so concerned about the levels of literacy that they have called in Debrett's, described in one report as 'the minders of Britons' Ps and Qs', to compile a guide on how to write proper e-mails.

I confess to being a regular e-mailer and, while I like its speed and convenience, it tends to run at the level of a scribbled note left out for the milkman. I was glad yesterday that a touch of a button sent some short messages to Australia, the USA and various parts of the UK, but I am not sure that meaningful relationships are built that way.

Mothering Sunday is traditionally a time for expressing love and thanks. Millions of pounds are spent in the process and no doubt the cards and gifts are gratefully received. But I am left wondering how many of those cards are simply the equivalent of a quick but emotional e-mail.

In contrast, a well-written letter can convey so much more. Beyond the words themselves lies the fact that someone has taken the time and trouble to sit and think about what to write. I am reminded that out of the 27 books of the New Testament, 21 were originally written as letters, and, a couple of millennia on, they are being read and reread to great profit.

Letters can be valuable and enriching, which makes me hope that the art of writing them will live on and grow stronger.

Mind you, as I know to my cost, not all letters are helpful. Henry Ward Beecher was a famous American preacher and author. Arriving at his church one Sunday morning, he found a letter addressed to him. Inside was a sheet of paper with one word written across it: 'Fool.'

He decided to share this rather unpleasant news with his congregation. He told them, 'I have known many an instance of a man writing a letter and forgetting to sign his name, but this is the only instance I have ever known of a man signing his name and forgetting to write the letter.'

## For further reading

1 CORINTHIANS 1:18–31

Letters can be revealing. Just before his mission to Corinth, Paul had been in Athens, where he had tried to convince people who 'spent their time doing nothing but talking about and listening to the latest ideas' (Acts 17:21). He had had very little success (v. 34), so he had come to Corinth 'resolved to know nothing while I was with you except Jesus Christ and him crucified' (1 Corinthians 2:2). His confidence had taken a knock (v. 3) and he had had to look again at his faith and realize that worldly wisdom gets in the way of men and women seeing the truth (1:20, 22).

In cultures where the sophisticated, the strong and the successful are admired, it's tough to stand up and declare your faith openly, both for Paul then and for us now. But we can encourage ourselves with Paul's words: 'For the foolishness of God is wiser than human wisdom, and the weakness of God is stronger than human strength' (1 Corinthians 1:25). We do not have to have persuasive arguments; we only have to tell the truth.

## Prayer

*I do not want to conform to the pattern of this world, Father, or value its wisdom over yours. Renew my mind, I pray.*

# Unfailing love

**The light shines in the darkness, but the darkness has not understood it.**
JOHN 1:5

One of the most harrowing experiences of my life was the day I visited Auschwitz. It is impossible to relate in words the dark, jagged feelings the place evokes. But, as always, slivers of light can be found.

Among the many stories of hope and heroism to emerge from this monument to human depravity is that of a priest, Father Maximilian Kolbe.

A rule of this hell hole was that any escape was punished by killing six randomly chosen prisoners. On one occasion, six men were dragged out before the ranks of prisoners.

Kolbe intervened with a passionate plea to the commanding officer. Pointing to one of the six, Franciszek Gajowniczek, Kolbe said, 'He's from my village. I know him. He is a good man and has a wife and several children. Take me instead. I am a priest with no family that needs me. Let me be punished in his place.'

The officer agreed, so Kolbe was taken and incarcerated in a punishment cell with the other men, where they were all slowly starved to death. If you visit Auschwitz today, you will see the cell that held Father Kolbe, with fresh flowers in it. Franciszek Gajowniczek survived the horror of Auschwitz and, after the war, moved his family close to the site of the camp. They made a solemn commitment to lay flowers in Father Kolbe's cell regularly, as an act of grateful remembrance.

In the Christian calendar, Lent is the period which runs up until Holy Saturday. Traditionally it has been a time for prayer, reflection and change. Some people find it helpful to give something up for the 40-

day period as a reminder that it is a special time, and as a link with Jesus' chosen fast in the desert after his baptism.

It's a good time to take stock of priorities and to listen extra keenly for the voice of God. But the greatest value of Lent, I believe, is that it offers the chance to hit a pause button in our over-busy, over-noisy, over-indulgent lives.

As the Gajowniczek family reminds us, remembrance is a special way to say 'thank you'. So perhaps a richer way of viewing Lent is not to see it as a time of giving something up reluctantly, but rather of laying something down gratefully—like fresh flowers.

## For further reading

LAMENTATIONS 3:17–42

It is hard to reconcile great evils that occur in our world, like the Holocaust, with the conviction that God is loving, kind, merciful and all-powerful. The writer of Lamentations describes scenes of utter horror (2:21; 4:10), in which even 'compassionate women' do un-speakable things in order to survive. The people of Jerusalem had rebelled against God, and defeat by their enemy was their punishment (3:42).

In this litany of the horrific conditions of those left behind in the devastated city, we might be surprised to find words like this: 'Because of the Lord's great love we are not consumed, for his compassions never fail. They are new every morning; great is your faithfulness' (3:22–23). It would have been understandable if Franciszek Gajowniczek had moved as far as possible from the scene of his suffering, but he did the opposite. Instead of wallowing in bitterness, he commemorated the greatest, most selfless gift that anyone could ever have given him. Even in the darkest places, God's light shines.

## Prayer

*Father God, I know that the suffering in the world brings you pain and that the day is coming when there will be no more suffering or pain because Jesus died in my place.*

27

# Passion and vision

Let us fix our eyes on Jesus, the author and perfecter of our faith, who for the joy set before him endured the cross, scorning its shame, and sat down at the right hand of the throne of God.
HEBREWS 12:2

The name Disney was in the news recently, with the opening of another Disneyland, this time in Hong Kong. Walt Disney's name has become synonymous with entertainment, and he is now as famous for his theme parks as for his movies.

Disney died in 1966 in St Joseph's Hospital, close by the famous Disney Studios in Burbank, California. The night before he passed away, an enterprising journalist secured permission to interview him, even though he was seriously ill and could barely talk. Disney asked the reporter to lie on the bed beside him so that he could whisper his replies to the questions.

The journalist wanted to know of his plans for the theme park that has now become the famous Disney World. The dying man drew an imaginary map on the ceiling above his bed and explained how he wanted the park to look. The rides, attractions, restaurants, gardens and lakes were painstakingly described. He shared his dream for something that, in fact, didn't open to the public for another six years.

A man who lay dying in hospital whispered into a reporter's ear for 30 minutes his vision for the future, knowing that he would not make it happen but others following behind would. I guess that is what it means to live with a vision and a passion.

Palm Sunday is the day when Christians recall Jesus arriving in Jerusalem amid much excitement from the crowds. Jesus knew that within a few short days the cheers would turn to jeers and that he would be betrayed, abandoned and crucified. But he had a greater plan in view.

The Bible explains his single-minded devotion in these words: 'Let us fix our eyes on Jesus, the author and perfecter of our faith, who for the joy set before him endured the cross, scorning its shame, and sat down at the right hand of the throne of God.'

Those words describe the greatest vision and passion the world has ever known. It's the dream of a redeemed humanity and a reconciled cosmos. And, if you read the Bible carefully, you can see that it makes way for a new order which, one day, will leave Mr Disney's theme parks standing.

## For further reading

GENESIS 37:1–11

A vision can have great power. Joseph's dreams of his family bowing down to him puffed him up so much that he became insufferable to his brothers, and even his doting father rebuked him (v. 10). Little did he imagine the trials he would suffer before what he had seen would be fulfilled. Before then, he had to go through the sheer terror of listening to his brothers discussing whether to kill him, the humiliation and powerlessness of being sold as a slave, the false allegation of attempted rape, and imprisonment with little hope of release. Each time there seemed some light at the end of the tunnel, his hopes were dashed.

Through these difficult years, perhaps Joseph's dreams sustained and encouraged him with the hope of seeing his family again and having a better future, but even in his wildest imagination he could not have foreseen the influence and prestige that he would eventually have. From a teenager who wanted to feel important in his family, he developed into a mature man who was able to discern God working out his purposes in other lives as well as his own, and to forgive past wrongs.

Has God given you a vision for your life? Are there still things you need to learn before you will be ready to fulfil it?

## Prayer

*Lord Jesus, you said that whoever could be trusted with very little could also be trusted with much. I want to be worthy of your trust, however and wherever you call me to serve you.*

# Freely given

*Written in March 2004, after the Madrid train bombing*

'I lay down my life—only to take it up again. No one takes it from me, but I lay it down of my own accord.'

JOHN 10:17–18

Evil is a talented actor. It would win a cluster of Oscars each year, if such a thing were possible. Evil can change its face, shape and form at will, but it can never change its nature.

Our hearts bleed today for the people of Spain in their grief. We embark on plans for our weekend while some fellow European lives are changed for ever. The dead and injured caught in the terrorist explosions in Madrid had made their plans for this weekend too, but today their calendars have been rewritten in a way that no one would want.

As I write, the shock is too fresh and the speculation too frenzied for the finger of blame to be pointed with any degree of certainty. Whatever badge this particular set of cruel killers hides behind, though, we all know who they work for ultimately. This was yet another grisly command performance of evil.

Those responsible may even claim some divine backing for their act of murder, but that is simply a symptom of their demonic madness. As the Pope declared within hours of the bombs exploding, 'These unjustifiable attacks are an offence to God.'

Prayers for those whose lives have been ripped apart will be offered across the world this weekend during this period known as Lent. It is a time when we remember Christ squaring up to the reality of evil through the temptation in the desert, as a prelude to challenging its false power through healing miracles of every sort. These were no magic tricks but a trailer for the kingdom to come, where evil is impotent.

Lent leads us to Easter and the crucifixion brought about (at one level) by an alliance of evil. But evil didn't win, because it was powerless to take Jesus' life. How can you rob someone of something they give freely? Jesus said, 'I lay down my life—only to take it up again. No one takes it from me, but I lay it down of my own accord. I have authority to lay it down and authority to take it up again' (John 10:17–18).

So in our grief we embrace hope. The days are numbered so far as evil is concerned, because the message of the empty cross of Jesus is that, there, evil did its worst and met its match.

## For further reading

JOHN 10:22–39; 18:1–11

In this first short passage in John's Gospel, Jesus twice appeared to be at the mercy of those who wished to destroy him (10:31, 39), but he slipped through their fingers. This was not the first time he had escaped violence in order to continue his work (Luke 4:28–30). Jesus was aware that his ministry would culminate in death, but only when the time was right. He referred to his death more and more explicitly to his disciples as time passed (see Mark 2:19–20; 9:9, 31), but they were too preoccupied, confused or unwilling to grasp fully what he was saying.

Jesus was in complete control as he sent Judas out to do what he had already decided to do (John 13:26–27), and then went out to the place where he knew Judas would expect to find him (18:2). He made no attempt to negotiate with the mob that had come to arrest him. Amazingly, when he first identified himself to them, 'they drew back and fell to the ground' (v. 6). Even at this late stage he could have escaped, but he chose instead to die for our sins.

# Prayer

*Behold the amazing sight!*
*The Saviour lifted high;*
*The Son of God, His soul's delight,*
*Expires in agony.*

*For us in love He bled,*
*For us in anguish died;*
*'Twas love that bowed his sacred head,*
*And pierced His precious side.*

PHILIP DODDRIDGE (1702–51)

# This I know

Without faith it is impossible to please God, because anyone who comes to him must believe that he exists and that he rewards those who earnestly seek him.

HEBREWS 11:6

There's a bumper sticker that reads, 'My mind's made up. Don't confuse me with the facts!' I was reminded of it a few days ago when I read about the fuss caused by, of all things, the discovery of the duck-billed platypus in the 19th century.

Apparently, when reports first filtered back from Australia about this curious creature, experts dismissed it as a hoax. The descriptions were, to put it mildly, unbelievable. The mystery animal was said to be furry, the size of a rabbit, with webbed feet and a bill like a duck. But the most extraordinary feature was the claim that it laid eggs, unlike any known mammal. To prove the animal's existence, a skin was sent for examination, but zoologists dismissed it. It took many years for the experts to budge.

Eventually, in 1884, a female platypus was shot after laying an egg and was found to have another egg in her body. The experts shifted their view and announced that the platypus was truly unique as an egg-laying mammal.

Not for the first time, the challenge to 'think outside the box' had been offered and spectacularly missed.

At Easter, millions gather around the globe to celebrate the death and resurrection of Jesus of Nazareth, two thousand years after he walked on planet earth. But the celebration provokes a huge dilemma. We know that dead men don't come back to life, so how can it be true that Jesus reversed a fundamental law of nature?

The stark answer offered by the Bible is that God raised Jesus to life. And if God wrote the laws that govern the universe, I guess that makes anything possible. But how can we know it's true and not a myth or a sentimental allegory designed to bring comfort, like a glass of warm milk on a cold night?

For me, the answer is wrapped up in two words: changed lives—the lives of those who first saw the risen Christ, as well as countless thousands through the generations, including cynics, mockers and rank unbelievers.

I saw a very sharp Easter card the other day. On the front was a simple line drawing of three crosses on a hill and the caption, 'They think it's all over.' Inside the card was a picture of an empty grave, the stone rolled back and the stark message, 'It is now!'

Easter offers the opportunity to wonder and worship, and discover that there is life outside the box.

## For further reading

HEBREWS 11:1–40

Reading through this list of 'faith heroes', we might feel discouraged about ourselves and our failures—unless we remind ourselves, for example, that Abraham tried to fulfil God's promise of numerous descendants his own way (Genesis 16:1–2), Moses was initially reluctant to do what God asked of him (Exodus 4:13), and Gideon's faith needed bolstering with several signs before he trusted God (Judges 6:17–22, 36–40). These were ordinary people called by God to do extraordinary things in his service. They didn't have all the answers but their lives were changed by faith in God.

God does not ask us to have blind faith in him; he helps us overcome our doubts and reveals himself to us if we 'earnestly seek him' (Hebrews 11:6). He provides us with many reasons to trust him and to believe that all things are possible with him. We have the evidence of the Bible, our own experience of God's provision and guidance, and the testimony of others about their changed lives, so that we can be 'sure of what we hope for and certain of what we do not see' (v. 1).

# Prayer

*I cannot tell how silently he suffered,*
*As with his peace he graced this place of tears,*
*Or how his heart upon the cross was broken,*
*The crown of pain to three and thirty years.*
*But this I know, he heals the broken-hearted,*
*And stays our sin, and calms our lurking fear,*
*And lifts the burden from the heavy laden,*
*For yet the Saviour, Saviour of the world is here.*

WILLIAM YOUNG FULLERTON (1857–1932)

# Good news for losers!

No, in all these things we are more than conquerors through
him who loved us.

ROMANS 8:37

How would you fancy making it into *The Guinness Book of Records*?
I guess most of us would feel a proud glow if we were nominated as
the world's best. But imagine how you'd feel if your record-breaking
achievement was actually based on a failure to achieve.

This is the likely fate of a Japanese racehorse called Haruurara, a
seven-year-old chestnut filly. She is a strong contender for being named
the world's worst racehorse, having never won a race in almost 100
outings. She has managed four second places in her career, which have
netted her owners a paltry £7000—barely enough to keep her in
carrots.

As an athlete, she doesn't have a great deal going for her. She is
agoraphobic, frightened by other horses, permanently scared and doesn't
eat much. Because of her social fears, she trains alone, either late at night
or early in the morning. Things became so bad that Haruurara looked
bound for the knacker's yard—and then the miracle occurred.

Somehow she became a star. A nationwide fan club was launched,
television stations took up her cause and the public swelled with pride
at a horse that epitomized the famous Japanese 'try harder' work ethic.
A highbrow Tokyo newspaper even wrote of Haruurara's dogged
determination as 'representing an alternative way in the era of corporate
restructuring'. Her face now appears on T-shirts and betting slips, as the
fever spreads. She stands every chance of becoming a legend, not for
being a winner but as a loser who never won a race.

The heroic Haruurara carries a timely message for Advent. Dr Luke,

37

in his Gospel, details the remarkable circumstances surrounding the birth of Jesus. In his opening chapters he describes some serious angelic overtime, two surprise pregnancies and a lot of astonished people.

Woven into the story are five songs, of which the most famous is probably Mary's heartfelt prayer of praise, often known as the Magnificat. It contains these words of wonder: God 'has brought down rulers from their thrones but has lifted up the humble. He has filled the hungry with good things but has sent the rich away empty' (Luke 1:52–53).

Good news for losers! What a great headline for Advent.

## For further reading

ROMANS 3:21–31

In a race, only one person (or horse) can come first and win. Very few people will find their names in *The Guinness Book of Records*, for that reason. Most of us won't even come second.

In one sense, though, we are all losers, as Paul points out: 'All have sinned and fall short of the glory of God' (v. 23). There are no exceptions, however talented or successful someone may be. If we are tempted to feel jealous of the success or wealth of others, let Jesus put things into perspective for us, when he says, 'What good is it for you to gain the whole world, yet forfeit your soul?' (Mark 8:36).

Without Christ, we are all losers, but in Christ 'we are more than conquerors' (Romans 8:37). Whoever we are, there's no need to be a loser. When it comes to eternal life, no one need miss out, because Jesus has won it for us.

## Prayer

*Thank you, heavenly Father, that you look beyond my worldly successes and failures, and beyond what I think of myself or what other people think of me, to who I really am—and you love me.*

# God of surprises

Jesus declared, 'I tell you the truth, no one can see the kingdom of God without being born again.'

JOHN 3:3

A small boy was writing a project on the subject of 'Families'. Seeking some background, he asked his mother how he had been born. Feeling flustered by the question, she told him that he had been delivered by a stork and left on the front doorstep.

The lad then phoned his grandmother and asked how his mum had come to be born. His grandmother, unsure about going into too much detail with the youngster, fobbed him off with a comment about her baby daughter being found under a gooseberry bush. 'What about you, Grandma?' the child pressed. 'Were you born in the same way?' 'That's right, dear,' she replied. 'In exactly the same way.'

The little boy sat down to write up his results. The opening sentence of his project read, 'In the last three generations there have not been any natural births in our family.'

As I write this, the annual season of carol services has begun. I attended my first this year at the chapel at Exeter University, as I joined faculty, students, staff and parents in a memorable celebration of the birth of the world's most remarkable person.

Despite the strange circumstances surrounding the coming of Jesus of Nazareth, his birth was thoroughly natural. He went through the same experience of entering the world that we all face. But here was no ordinary child. In the majestic opening words of John's Gospel, 'The Word became flesh and made his dwelling among us' (1:14)—or, as a more exact translation reads, 'he pitched his tent with us'.

That is both the miracle and the mystery of the incarnation. God did not abandon us or leave us to our own devices, but sent his own Son to bring lost children home.

Writing many centuries ago, Iraeneus summed up this good news in a memorable way: 'The Word of God, on account of his great love for mankind, became what we are in order to make us what he is himself.'

Standing in the candlelight of the university church a few nights ago, I felt a fresh sense of wonder that God has not lost his capacity to surprise us. After all, the incarnation of Jesus Christ took the world so much by storm that the shock waves reverberate 2000 years on.

In all the busyness and rush of the season, leave room for God to surprise you.

## For further reading

ACTS 2:22–41

For three thousand of Peter's listeners in Jerusalem on the Day of Pentecost, the realization that the man they had crucified was God's long-awaited Messiah cut them 'to the heart' (v. 37). They weren't persuaded just intellectually; they were inwardly, painfully convicted. What were they to do? Peter told them to change direction ('repent') and demonstrate their desire to follow Jesus by being baptized, both as a witness to those around them and to affirm to themselves that they had been washed clean of their sin. And the promise for them and future generations of followers was 'the gift of the Holy Spirit' (v. 38).

The message hasn't changed since then, although countless lives have been changed by the message. By his Holy Spirit, God has made his spiritual dwelling with those he has called (v. 39), accompanying us on the journey, giving guidance and the power to serve him in ordinary and extraordinary ways, bringing blessing through difficulty, always equipping and providing, never letting us down. We need to go on repenting when we fall, being renewed as we ask daily to be filled with the Spirit, and recalling frequently and with thankfulness the day when we first knew God and he began to surprise us.

## Prayer

*Holy Spirit, fill me again. Come in power and overwhelm me. Come quietly and comfort me. You know my deepest need.*

# The reason for the season

*Written in December 1998*

The people walking in darkness have seen a great light; on those living in the land of the shadow of death a light has dawned.
Isaiah 9:2

The other morning, I bumped into a friend who was wearing a badge. Thinking it was his birthday, I stopped to congratulate him, only to discover that the message on the badge read, 'Jesus, the Reason for the Season'. It was a helpful reminder in a frantic week.

It was a reminder that Birmingham City Council could do with, following their controversial decision to abandon the word 'Christmas' in favour of 'Winterval' (an odd sounding non-word if ever there was one), in the belief that it would cause less offence to those of other faiths or no faith at all.

All over the world this coming week, millions will gather to celebrate the birth of the one who put the Christ into Christmas, but the good news is not limited to the faithful. As the Bible says, 'The true light that gives light to everyone was coming into the world' (John 1:9). This is not light for the select, churchgoing few, but light for all who want to stop stumbling around in the dark.

There is a famous piece of writing entitled 'One Solitary Life'. It outlines something of the wonder at Bethlehem that made heaven sing.

*He was born in an obscure village, the son of a peasant woman. He grew up in yet another village where he worked in a carpenter's shop till he was thirty. Then for three years he was an itinerant preacher.*

*He never wrote a book. He never held an office. He never had a family or* owned a house. He didn't go to college. He never visited a big city. He never travelled more than 200 miles from the place where he was born. He did none of the things one usually associates with greatness. He had no credential but himself.

He was only 33 when the tide of public opinion turned against him. His friends ran away. He was nailed to a cross between two thieves. While he was dying, his executioners gambled for his clothing, the only property he had on earth.

Nineteen centuries have come and gone and today he is the central figure of the human race. All the armies that ever marched, all the navies that ever sailed, all the parliaments that ever sat, all the kings that ever reigned, put together, have not affected the life of man on this earth as much as that one solitary life.

## For further reading

LUKE 2:8–20

Are you the kind of person who, when you read a novel, are tempted to read the last page before you have finished the book, just to see how it all turns out? When it comes to the Christmas story, we already know what is going to happen, but the shepherds back then had yet to see the story unfold. In fact, they were part of the story. It was a never-to-be-forgotten night. First, angels disturbed their night-time vigil; then they hurried into Bethlehem, which was heaving with visitors and, almost certainly, was not the still and silent place described in Christmas carols. They found the grubby stable and saw the baby, God's hope for the world, in the helplessness, vulnerability and wonder of very new life. God's Messiah was born not into royalty or a noble family but to a very ordinary couple without the influence or money to get a proper bed for the night.

More than 2000 years later, we know much more about how Jesus lived and died and rose again, but still the story hasn't ended. Like the shepherds, we too are part of it.

## Prayer

*Mighty God, Everlasting Father, Prince of Peace, help us to appreciate afresh the wonder of the first Christmas and the baby who was born to be the Saviour of the world.*

# Change

# A new beginning

So if the Son sets you free, you will be free indeed.
JOHN 8:36

September is a month of change. Changes in the season are coupled with change at home, school and college. With that in mind, let me pass on a story that fits the 'changing gear' theme.

When President Bill Clinton first met Nelson Mandela, they shared a memorable conversation. Clinton asked a searching question. 'When you were released from prison, Mr Mandela, I woke my daughter at three o'clock in the morning. I wanted her to see this historic event. As you marched from the cell block across the yard to the gate of the prison, the camera focused in on your face. I have never seen such anger, and even hatred, in any man as was expressed on your face at that time. That's not the Nelson Mandela I know today. What was that all about?'

Mandela replied, 'I'm surprised that you saw that, and I regret that the cameras caught my anger. As I walked across that courtyard that day I thought to myself, "They've taken everything from you that matters. Your cause is dead. Your family is gone. Your friends have been killed. Now they're releasing you, but there is nothing left for you out there." Then I sensed an inner voice saying to me, "Nelson! For 27 years you were their prisoner but you were always a free man! Don't allow them to make you a free man, only to turn you into their prisoner!"'

The skill of moving forward is found in learning to put the past behind us. It may be finding the ability to forgive someone, or letting go of the consuming desire for revenge. It may mean leaving some questions unanswered by recognizing that worrying won't provide the answer. For some, it means learning to stop looking over our shoulders and constantly thinking, 'If only…'

Notice, the next time you see a photograph or film clip of Nelson Mandela, how the answer is written all over his lived-in face. That smile and infectious laugh, the sense of peace that oozes outwards, they are the evidence of someone who has turned the page and started a new chapter.

They are the marks of a man who is *truly* free.

## For further reading

JOHN 5:1–15

Perhaps, when you read this passage, you were surprised that Jesus should have asked the man, 'Do you want to get well?' 'Why wouldn't he?' we might ask. But after 38 years he had become established in a certain pattern of life that revolved around waiting for the water to be stirred (v. 7). Change might have seemed quite threatening. Today we might describe him as 'institutionalized'.

It is logical to assume that the man's problem was that he couldn't walk, because Jesus told him to pick up his mat and walk, but in another healing in the Bible it is stated explicitly that the person was paralysed (Matthew 9:6; Mark 2:10; Luke 5:24). Maybe this man's need for help in getting into the pool came more from the inevitable weakness associated with lying on his mat day after day than from an inability to walk. Jesus' words in verse 14 suggest there was more to his illness than a simple physical explanation. Whatever his problem may have been, though, when he picked up his mat and walked, it was a new beginning for him.

Is God calling you to make a change in your life? Is there some action you can take or a symbolic way you can mark the leaving behind of the old and the beginning of the new in your life?

## Prayer

*Meditate on God's kindness, that he often asks us to make changes one step at a time and that he always equips those he calls.*

# Things can only get better!

*Written in April 2004*

Blessed are those whose help is the God of Jacob, whose hope is in the Lord their God... the Lord, who remains faithful for ever.
PSALM 146:5–6

Unless 26 April 1994 was a special day in your life, it probably passed like any other Saturday in early spring. For me, it marked the first appearance of this column, on a trial run; and today, the tenth anniversary, it's time to hang up the word processor, so to speak. This summer I take up a new post in an international church in Geneva. The next few months will involve preparations for that move, so the tenth birthday seems a good place to stop.

Reflecting on the experience, about 500 columns on, I recognize some lessons learnt along the way. Foremost in my mind is how kind people can be. The occasional angry letter has been far outweighed by the ones that ask a question, make a point or simply say thanks. Then there are dozens of personal contacts that usually begin, 'You look much better than your photograph.' You'll never know how good that makes me feel!

A second lesson is how much you can pack into 390 words when you try—and for someone who constantly struggles to be a better communicator, that has proved invaluable.

I am also grateful for the opportunity provided by *The Western Morning News* to offer comment on the news from a religious perspective. For those who have an inbuilt mistrust of the media, it's worth recording that I have enjoyed a free hand in what is written and the only changes made have been to improve style rather than change substance.

Before this begins to sound like an acceptance speech at the Oscars,

I need to draw a line, but I can't do that without acknowledging the part played by my life-partner Ruth, who usually listens to every column before it's submitted. The occasional, 'You can't say that!' has kept me safe, you calm, and the paper still in business.

I sign off with the story of a minister who announced his impending departure to his shocked congregation. At the end of the service, a woman in obvious distress shook his hand as she left. The minister offered some comfort. 'Didn't you hear what I said about trusting the Lord to send a good man to replace me?'

'Yes,' the woman sobbed, 'I heard all right. But that's what they said last time!'

## For further reading

PSALM 146

Experience teaches us that change is not always for the better. That's why some people are so averse to and frightened of it. Even if their current situation is not that good, at least it's familiar. When something comes to an end, or when we celebrate an anniversary, we are reminded that time is passing. As we get older, there may be a sense of the diminishing of our opportunities and abilities, of regret for things we might have done differently but now cannot alter.

The Bible is a realistic book. Its characters are shown doing great things for God as well as abjectly failing. They are people just like us. But the Bible is also a profoundly hopeful book. The writer of Psalm 146 says, 'The Lord... remains faithful forever' (v. 6) and 'The Lord reigns forever' (v. 10). Change is inevitable at various stages of our lives, but we know that our God is faithful and that he is in control.

## Prayer

*Unchangeable God, in the uncertainties of life I turn to you, knowing that you are wholly trustworthy. You know already what the rest of today will hold for me and where I will be in a week, a month, even years from now. You are my hope, my comforter and my encourager, and I praise you.*

# There has to be a pony

And now these three remain: faith, hope and love. But the greatest
of these is love.
1 CORINTHIANS 13:13

There were two brothers who were complete opposites: one was a total
pessimist and the other an uncrushable optimist. One Christmas, their
parents decided to play a game. For the pessimist, they assembled a
stack of toys in brightly coloured parcels and waited to see if he would
respond true to type.

He sat, surrounded by his new toys, with not a glimmer of a smile
on his face. When asked if he liked the expensive gifts, he moaned,
'They'll probably all get broken, and as for the stereo, I don't have any
CDs anyway.'

The optimistic son was given a single box with no wrapping
whatsoever. When his turn came, he opened the lid to discover a
shovelful of horse manure. A large grin broke across his face as he
shouted, 'Do you see what I've got? There has got to be a pony round
here somewhere!'

I have a friend who tells that story and concludes with the line, 'You
can always tell the optimists. They are the ones who, no matter what
gets dumped on them, can still shout, "There's a pony out there
somewhere!"'

As the political party conference season comes round each year,
there is the usual interesting mix of optimism and pessimism around.
But is our outlook on life simply a reflection of temperament? Do we
have to stick with how we are programmed or can pessimists sometimes look on the bright side and optimists occasionally acknowledge
that some clouds come minus silver lining?

Hope is one of the three great words of the Christian faith, the others being faith and love. Hope is seen as more than a wistful wish: it is a solid anchor that holds us steady when the storm is at its height. Hope is a quiet confidence, which says that even when we don't know what the future holds, we can trust the one who holds the future.

There is a prayer of blessing in the Bible about hope: 'May the God of hope fill you with all joy and peace as you trust in him, so that you may overflow with hope by the power of the Holy Spirit' (Romans 15:13).

The gift is not just for one type of personality. It's for all. And, as Winnie the Pooh fans will understand, that even includes the Eeyores among us.

## For further reading

2 CORINTHIANS 4:1–18

Twice in this chapter Paul declares, 'We do not lose heart' (vv. 1, 16). He does not mention the word 'hope' but hope permeates the passage. He tells the Corinthian church that he and his companions are 'hard pressed on every side… perplexed… persecuted… struck down… outwardly wasting away' (vv. 8–9, 16) but that these are 'light and momentary troubles' outweighed by the 'eternal glory' on which they have set their hopes (v. 17).

Sometimes our troubles overwhelm us, leaving us feeling hopeless and despairing. When we don't have the resources in ourselves to be optimistic, hope is God's gift to us, along with a different perspective on the meaning of the trials we undergo. We do not have to manufacture this hope for ourselves or talk ourselves into a hopeful mood. We can ask the 'God of hope' to fill us by his Holy Spirit with 'joy and peace', and hope will be the overflow of this (Romans 15:13). Our troubles may not disappear but our outlook on them will be transformed.

## Prayer

*Lord God, fill me with joy and peace as I trust in you, so that I may overflow with hope by the power of your Holy Spirit. In Jesus' name I ask this.*

# Worth it!

Look, he is coming with the clouds, and every eye will see him, even those who pierced him; and all the peoples of the earth will mourn because of him.

REVELATION 1:7

I am looking at a photograph of a man with no hands. He's kneeling on the floor, with one of his bare feet pressing down on a piece of paper, and from the size of his grin you'd think he'd won the lottery.

His name is Ismail Daramy and he lives in Sierra Leone, where civil war has wrecked the country for the past decade. Ismail is grinning because he has just recorded his vote in a democratic election to choose a government. He has voted with his big toe. He had to do it that way because they cut off his hands the last time he voted.

Ismail, along with others in his village, voted for the wrong side, so they taught him a lesson by cutting off his hands. Some people lost their ears or lips; others had their eyes gouged out. Apparently, the queue at polling stations in the latest election was a remarkable sight as lines of maimed people stood patiently in line to exercise their right to vote.

A journalist watched as Ismail waited his turn and was helped out of his shoe and sock by an election official. Using the stubs at the ends of his arms, he carried the precious ballot slip to the booth, where another official placed an ink pad on the floor. With a defiant grin, Ismail placed his inky toe on the paper alongside the name of the same candidate he had voted for in 1996—only this time no one could punish or threaten him. Here was a man who was free to choose, choosing to be free.

Ismail had been practising for weeks because he didn't want to get it wrong and spoil his paper. Some of his countrymen and women waited for hours to vote, many arriving at one in the morning to get a place in the queue.

I feel a cocktail of emotions as I read Ismail's story. Anger and admiration vie for first place, but it's the nagging feeling of sheer embarrassment that pips them both to the post. I am ashamed at taking for granted what others would die for. Listen to Ismail's words: 'I have suffered for democracy. I lost my hands, my job, my home. I beg to feed my family.'

God give us the ability to cherish, not squander, privilege.

## For further reading

JOHN 19:16–37

The scars of Ismail and others in Sierra Leone demonstrate graphically and horrifically the price they have paid for democratic freedoms that we in this country rarely give a thought to. They also demonstrate the value these people place on their freedoms. Jesus paid a price in suffering that we can only begin to imagine, when he died on the cross for our sins, and his scars demonstrate the value he places on each one of us.

John's account records the petty dramas playing out beneath the cross as Jesus hung there painfully dying: the squabble between the chief priests and Pilate, the soldiers sharing out Jesus' clothes. Everyday life continued as the most momentous event of human history took place. In the frustrations and distractions of ordinary, daily life, do we ever neglect to feel grateful for the freedoms we enjoy, both because we live in a democratic country and because we are citizens of a heavenly kingdom (Philippians 3:20)? And when it comes to exercising the rights that we have, are we conscientious and thoughtful in doing so?

## Prayer

*Ask God to meet the practical needs of those, like Ismail, whose desire to have a say in how they are governed has cost them dearly. Remember before God those who are in prison or suffering loss right now because they have spoken up for human rights and the freedom to choose.*

# Too valuable to be thrown away

Bear in mind that our Lord's patience means salvation.
2 PETER 3:15

I was helping with a building project yesterday when a friend asked me to pass him his disposable saw. I was surprised to discover that such things existed. In the past, a craftsman would have owned one set of tools throughout his career, but now we tend to throw things away because it's cheaper than repairing them.

I know it's a huge jump from disposable tools to the state of society, but I suspect there are a few connections to be made.

If we learn that it is cheaper to buy a new one than fix the old one, then this principle will be applied in other areas, too. For example, a world that has provided us with disposable nappies and throwaway watches has also become a place of insecure jobs and uncertain relationships. The carpenter who kept his tools for life would probably have worked for the same boss all his life as well.

The word 'patience' occurs in the Bible many times. The old King James Version translates the word as 'longsuffering', which to me seems a sharper description. Longsuffering is an unknown quantity in a disposable world, because it implies that some things are too valuable to be thrown away. The more you work for something, the more it is prized. When you struggle hard to hold a relationship together, it shows the other person that you think they are worth the effort.

Let me quote a few examples where longsuffering has paid off:

- In its first year, the Coca Cola company sold only 400 bottles of Coke.
- In its first year, the Gillette company sold only 51 razors and 168 blades.

- A boy was thrown out of his Latin class. As a result, he made up his mind to excel in English. His name was Winston Churchill.
- A six-year-old was sent home from school with a note saying he was too stupid to learn. He was Thomas Edison.
- Sir Walter Scott's teacher believed him to be a hopeless dunce.
- Louis Pasteur was considered to be the slowest boy in his chemistry class.

Henry Ward Beecher defined the difference between perseverance and obstinacy: one often comes with a strong will, and the other with a strong won't.

Some of life's greatest achievements come about only after a long, hard slog. 'Use once and throw it away' may herald a great convenience in the kitchen but it's a flawed philosophy for living.

## For further reading

GENESIS 1

Is it only today that there is the desire to have everything instantly, or were previous ages characterized by the same kind of impatience? When we want immediate results, we may lose out on quality if we don't take care. God is not like that: he is caring and careful. We see this exemplified in his creation of the world—and it is his world, not ours, as we so often designate it. Meticulously he designed and made each part, first establishing the foundations, until he 'saw that it was good' (v. 10), and then the details, until finally he 'created human beings in his own image... male and female' (v. 27).

When God's much-loved, carefully designed creation wilfully went wrong, he was prepared to pay the price of repairing the relationship. 'He is patient with [us], not wanting anyone to perish, but everyone to come to repentance' (2 Peter 3:9). And he continues to be patient with us as we mess up and fail time after time, transforming us 'into his likeness with ever-increasing glory' (2 Corinthians 3:18), until the day when we see him face to face and are no longer able to sin.

## Prayer

*Creator of the universe and my heavenly Father, help me to be patient with other people as you are patient with me. When I am tempted to become impatient with people or situations, remind me that, through them, I can learn to be more like you.*

# Take My Life

*Take my life, and let it be*
*Consecrated, Lord, to Thee;*
*Take my moments and my days,*
*Let them flow in ceaseless praise.*

*Take my hands and let them move*
*At the impulse of Thy love;*
*Take my feet and let them be*
*Swift and beautiful for Thee.*

*Take my silver and my gold,*
*Not a mite would I withhold;*
*Take my intellect, and use*
*Every power as Thou shalt choose.*

*Take my voice, and let me sing*
*Always, only for my King;*
*Take my lips and let them be*
*Filled with messages from Thee.*

*Take my will and make it Thine;*
*It shall be no longer mine:*
*Take my heart, it is Thine own;*
*It shall be Thy royal throne.*

*Take my love; my Lord, I pour*
*At Thy feet its treasure-store:*
*Take myself, and I will be*
*Ever, only, all for Thee!*

FRANCES RIDLEY HAVERGAL (1836–79)

# Take my life

Who despises the day of small things?
ZECHARIAH 4:10

'Small is beautiful.' Schumacher (the economist, not the racing driver!) coined this phrase in the title of a book—and it's a phrase worth considering in a world that often suggests that bigger equals better.

Last weekend I had the privilege of visiting the village of Madron near Penzance. I'd been invited to attend the annual 'feast' celebrations and speak at two special church services.

The feast focuses on one of the Cornish saints, Madern, and his faithful work in bringing the Christian message to Cornwall. I was unsure what to expect. After all, some commemorative events have long passed their sell-by dates. But I was treated to a warm welcome and some fascinating insights into 21st-century Cornish life.

I learnt three special lessons from my day.

First, it's important to remember our roots. In the words of Isaiah the prophet, 'Look to the rock from which you were cut and to the quarry from which you were hewn' (Isaiah 51:1). It's true that we sometimes make history mean what we want it to mean, and are guilty of romanticizing or even fabricating its story. But a generation that knows where it comes from is more likely to have a clearer idea of where it is heading.

Second, community life is a gift to be treasured. On my drive through Cornwall, I tuned into a radio programme on which pundits bemoaned the loss of a sense of community in many parts of Britain. My day turned up a few clues to how we can find what's missing. Most of us are aware of the huge changes in Cornish life and the devastating effects that have followed the closure of mines and the wholesale disruption of traditional ways of life in fishing and agriculture. But I discovered a community wanting to stand together rather than fall apart; if anything, the hardships have made their sense of belonging even greater.

Third, unity works best from the bottom up. For the feast day, it's a case of church in the morning and chapel in the evening, with both congregations supporting each other. The common purpose was to offer worship to Jesus Christ as Saviour and Lord. In other words, this was a unity of the heart rather than a marriage of convenience.

Three lessons from a Cornish village.

Small really is beautiful—as another village, called Bethlehem, once proved.

## For further reading

JOHN 6:5–13; LUKE 21:1–4; ISAIAH 51:1–2

In the hands of God, acts of unselfishness and obedience can have great significance. One boy's generous offer to share his lunch fed five thousand people. A poor woman, giving unostentatiously the very little that she had to live on, did not go unremarked by Jesus and she is still held up as an example to us. A whole nation, God's chosen people, began with an elderly couple called Abraham and Sarah.

Many small acts begin and end small, and only God takes note of them, but how exciting it is to think that something we do in obedience to God's prompting could lead to much bigger outcomes. Therefore, we should live thoughtfully, moment by moment, offering our abilities and opportunities to God, never discounting the importance of small things.

## Prayer

*Take my life, and let it be*
*Consecrated, Lord, to Thee;*
*Take my moments and my days,*
*Let them flow in ceaseless praise.*

# Take my feet

Those whose walk is blameless and who do what is righteous...
Those who do these things will never be shaken.

PSALM 15:2, 5

I tuned into the BBC's *Best of British* the other evening, when the subject was the 'Peter Pan of pop', Sir Cliff Richard. It charted a career spanning 40 years and acknowledged his outstanding contribution to the entertainment industry.

I was pleased to see that the programme rejected blandness and mentioned the critics, including those radio stations that steadfastly refuse to play Sir Cliff's records. Cliff himself confessed astonishment that his music was not treated on the grounds of merit but rejected simply because his name was attached to the label. He cited a recent ploy, when he released a record under a pseudonym: the stations loved it and subsequently played it.

It was a good programme but it left me confused. In any other country in the world, someone with Cliff Richard's track record would be heralded from the rooftops. So why, in certain sections of the media, is he given such a hard time?

I suspect that his squeaky-clean image may have something to do with it. If he had a foul mouth or a drink problem, was into drugs or was found to be a serial adulterer, some people would like him more. How sad.

I have met Sir Cliff a few times and, although I have never been a big fan of his music, I admire him as a man. From my experience, what you see in public is what you get in private—a thoroughly nice guy whose success lies in the fact that he has never believed his own publicity.

Long before it was fashionable for pop stars to get involved in famine relief, Cliff was working quietly behind the scenes, giving time and energy to Third World development. His work over the years has raised millions of pounds for the poorest people in the world.

A couple of friends of mine travelled with him to eastern Europe to look at some projects he has helped. They reported the same story—of a man keen to express his Christian faith in practical action, someone who sees his privileged position as a responsibility rather than a luxury.

The best comment on Cliff the other evening came from Olivia Newton John. 'Some people talk the talk,' she said, 'but he walks the walk.'

That says more than anything the cynics can throw at him. Rock on, Cliff. And keep letting your actions do the talking.

## For further reading

MATTHEW 25:34–40; JAMES 2:14–17

In these verses from the letter of James, he is not saying that we have to do certain things in order to be saved. As Paul says, 'It is by grace you have been saved, through faith… not by works' (Ephesians 2:8–9). Eternal life is God's free and undeserved gift to us. What James is pointing out is the absurdity of a faith that doesn't make a difference to the way we live. When Olivia Newton John said that Cliff Richard 'walks the walk', she was talking about the way his actions line up with what he says he believes.

A true, living faith in Jesus will affect the way we live. We are not compelled to prove our faith by what we do, but it is when we seek to do what is right, to be consistent and serve others, that our faith is authenticated. What is more, when we show kindness to anyone at all, it is as though we are doing it for Jesus (Matthew 25:40).

## Prayer

*Take my hands and let them move*
*At the impulse of Thy love;*
*Take my feet and let them be*
*Swift and beautiful for Thee.*

# Take my gifts

[Remember] the words the Lord Jesus himself said:
'It is more blessed to give than to receive.'

ACTS 20:35

A few days ago, I was given a priceless present. I sit here looking at it now, wondering if I'm worth it. It's a picture calendar, emblazoned with the name of a chain of chemist's shops, most of it incomprehensible to me as it's written in Portuguese.

Last week, I walked through the slums of Sao Paulo, Brazil, one of the world's top five mega-cities and home to 20 million people. Estimates vary as to how many of these people live in favelas—shanty towns that have sprung up wherever there is a spare parcel of land.

In contrast to their surroundings, favela dwellers are bright, cheerful people who make guests feel welcome. In spite of frequent incidents of drug dealing and violence, people are doing their level best to maintain a quality and dignity of life. I saw some excellent work being undertaken by various agencies, particularly churches who offer much more than hymns and hallelujahs.

My special gift came at the end of a sticky day of visits. We were welcomed into a small shack, which was home to mum, dad and three children. The youngest, Veronica, suffered from encephalomyelitis—acute inflammation of the brain and spinal cord. Aged just two years, her prospects were bleak.

Mum and dad talked in an almost abstract way about Veronica's constant fevers and inability to feed. They were curious about Britain and, through our interpreter, plied us with questions about pop music, Tottenham Hotspur and Sherlock Holmes. The man of the house was acutely embarrassed that they had no coffee or food to offer. It was a bad time, he explained, making me wonder what on earth a good time meant.

And then, the calendar. He pointed to it hanging in pride of place in the middle of the wall. (It was the only decoration on any of the plywood walls in the whole shack.) Before I could protest, he was on his feet, unhitching it from the rusty nail and handing it to me with a grin of pleasure.

Thank you, my Brazilian friend, for a gift I treasure, but even more for reminding me of a question that has haunted me for 30-something years. How come those from whom you expect so much come up with the least, while those from whom you expect nothing give the most?

## For further reading

Exodus 35:30—36:7

Sermons on giving are frequently preceded by an apology for bringing up the subject. When people ask how much they should give to God's work, and tithing is suggested, the question might arise of whether to tithe the gross amount before tax or the net amount. What an amazing story this is, then: the people had to be 'restrained from bringing more' (36:6)! How often today, in the affluent West, do we see this situation?

There are occasions, though, when a group of Christians gets a vision from God for something that requires generous, even sacrificial, giving and discovers the excitement of being able to be a part of it. And, as the Israelites realized, giving is about more than money; they could donate their skills and abilities too (v. 1). So let's give without begrudging and serve God willingly with the skills and abilities he has given us. Then we shall find out, if we haven't already, that 'it is more blessed to give than to receive' (Acts 20:35).

### Prayer

*Take my silver and my gold,*
*Not a mite would I withhold;*
*Take my intellect, and use*
*Every power as Thou shalt choose.*

# Take my lips

If you confess with your mouth, 'Jesus is Lord,' and believe in your
heart that God raised him from the dead, you will be saved.

ROMANS 10:9

My life is never dull. I recently spent a day in London, making a film for
a charity. I had been asked to present a short report of their work, along
the lines of 'Look at some of the ways the money you've given has been
used…'.

The trouble was that one person had written the script, another
person had checked it for accuracy on behalf of the charity, then a third
individual had edited it to fit the filming schedule. By the time it arrived
with me, it looked like a report from a multi-lingual committee of
scientists on organic worm farming in the Shetlands.

I felt like David about to fight Goliath. If you remember the story,
Saul insisted on giving David his own armour to wear, for maximum
protection. But David opted for the weapons he knew best: a few
stones and a catapult. His job as a shepherd meant that the armour
made him feel weighed down and clumsy, when he needed speed and
freedom of movement.

Anyway, I pleaded my case successfully and ended up with a script
in my own words. The clinching moment came when I pointed out that
the script instructed the presenter to be 'warm, passionate and sincere'.
For me, at eight o'clock in the morning, that's a tall order, but the best
chance I had of achieving all three qualities was to speak my own words
and not someone else's.

We can all spot insincerity a mile off. Interestingly, we even use the
phrase 'He's reading from a script' if we feel that someone is not
speaking from the heart. For a speech to come across as real, we need

more than words: a person's being needs to be behind the words.

Most of us have witnessed someone saying all the right things but not in the right way. Somehow, nothing adds up when the speaker's heart is not in it. Jesus illustrated this in an uncomfortable confrontation when some religious leaders questioned his integrity. For those who take their Jesus meek and mild, his reply is astonishingly straight: 'You brood of vipers, how can you who are evil say anything good? For out of the overflow of the heart the mouth speaks' (Matthew 12:34).

Our words, you see, are the window of our souls.

## For further reading

MATTHEW 12:33–37; PSALM 63

Although we may often describe words we regret having said as 'thoughtless', Jesus and the psalmist David are in agreement that our words are the fruit of what we have stored up in ourselves. David has seen God at work (Psalm 63:2); he has thought about him through long nights (v. 6); he has seen his dependence on God justified (v. 8). When we spend a lot of time with another person, we may find ourselves using the same turns of phrase, or even unconsciously mimicking our friend's accent or intonation. Without even noticing, we become like our friends.

In a similar way, if we want to become more like Jesus, we need to spend time with him. Then, when we speak, we won't have to make too much of an effort to watch what we say, because our hearts will overflow naturally with the good we have stored up.

## Prayer

*Take my voice, and let me sing*
*Always, only for my King;*
*Take my lips and let them be*
*Filled with messages from Thee.*

# Take my will

I wait for the Lord, my soul waits, and in his word I put my hope.
PSALM 130:5

Waiting is never easy. I have an inbuilt aversion to it, mainly due to a childhood spent constantly hanging around adults while longing, like a labrador, to be let out for a run.

Even the famous carol 'Once in royal David's city' sent a shudder down my young spine. There's a verse that describes the prospect of heaven, summarized in the words 'When like stars his children crowned, all in white shall wait around.' Well, for this ten-year-old boy, being dressed all in white was not a major turn-on but the thought of an eternity just waiting around was a million times worse.

But as I have grown older and picked up a few insights on the journey, I have learned and am learning how important waiting can sometimes prove to be. For instance, I discovered that a nine-month pregnancy is an important preparation time for parents. I have also found that to wait for something by saving, working hard or turning the impatience of longing into a positive force for good can help to build character.

The Bible has a great deal to say on the subject of patience, which is hardly surprising, because faith is often a waiting game. Frederick W. Faber summed it up when he wrote, 'We must wait for God, long, meekly, in the wind and wet, in the thunder and lightning, in the cold and dark. Wait, and he will come. He never comes to those who do not wait.'

I have been going through a waiting period in my life of late and, although difficult, it has been a time of rich reward. Here are a few pages from the catalogue of benefits. It develops trust in God, teaches you to pray with greater feeling, and opens your mind and heart to the needs of others stuck in a waiting room too. It reminds you of life's Really Important Things, it strengthens and deepens friendships, and you discover afresh that none of us runs the universe.

I could go on, but instead I would like to offer three (slow) cheers for waiting. Oh yes, and to remind myself as much as anyone else, 'Wait for the Lord; be strong and take heart and wait for the Lord' (Psalm 27:14).

## For further reading

PSALM 40

We're not told what events in David's life this psalm refers to, but it is interesting that it is written in the waiting time between asking God for help and seeing his prayer answered. David affirms that God has heard him (v. 1). God has not yet delivered David from his enemies, but rather has given him a new assurance. David may have been slipping into 'the slimy pit' of doubt but God has 'set [his] feet on a rock' and given him 'a new song' so that 'many will see and fear and put their trust in the Lord' (v. 3) as they see David's example. In David's waiting time, God has blessed him and others through him. As he recalls God's faithfulness in the past, he reaffirms his desire to conform his will to God's will (v. 8).

In verses 13–17, David returns to his problems and prays, 'Be pleased, O Lord, to save me; O Lord, come quickly to help me… O my God, do not delay.' But God has already led him further along the path of discipleship. We can learn from David that waiting time is not wasted time if we are willing to see it as an opportunity for growth rather than as an obstacle.

## Prayer

*Take my will and make it Thine;*
*It shall be no longer mine:*
*Take my heart, it is Thine own;*
*It shall be Thy royal throne.*

# Take my love

*Written in September 2003*

'Why are you bothering her? She has done a beautiful thing to me.'
MARK 14:6

If you are thinking of a late summer break, I have an interesting suggestion. Grab a few days in the Italian sunshine and visit the remote village of Trasacco, where you will see a very odd sight. Don't worry about finding the village. Most people in Italy will tell you where it is, since it has hit the headlines big time.

Trasacco became famous overnight because the villagers have locked their priest in his church and are refusing to let him out. They haven't done this because they don't like him; on the contrary, they like him so much that they won't let him leave.

Father Emilio Succhhiella is a Franciscan monk who serves as the village priest, but he is the last monk in the monastery and his superiors have decided to close the place down for good. Father Emilio said his farewells last week with great sadness and then discovered that he had a revolting flock. They wouldn't let him go and forced him back into the church building.

The astonished priest watched as villagers bolted, barred and padlocked every door and window in the church and then set to work on bricking up the main doorway with breezeblocks. The locals see the decision to close the monastery as an attack on their faith and are determined not to lose their much-loved parish priest. At their insistence, Father Emilio is continuing to conduct services and, as villagers gather outside in the square, he pushes communion bread and wine to them through a grille.

I read an interview with the stunned priest a few days ago in which he shared his total surprise at the militant stand of the village. Yet he was deeply touched by their care for him and the lengths to which they would go to keep him at the heart of their little community. One phrase from the interview lives with me: 'I am a prisoner of love,' he said.

Love makes us do crazy things, inspires heroic efforts and sometimes demands a bold demonstration. These strange goings-on in a usually sleepy village left me with a pair of daunting thoughts. How special it must be to be loved like that, and how important it is to express what we feel while we have the chance.

Viva Italia!

## For further reading

MARK 14:3–9

Sandwiched between descriptions of the plotting against Jesus, as events march inexorably towards his death, we read this surprising story of what was, for the observers, a rather embarrassing incident. Hence their sudden concern for the poor! The woman came with her most expensive and treasured possession and poured it all out. Her gesture could not have been more extravagant or more public, and we can have no doubt about how much she loved Jesus, who did not allow himself to be sidetracked into a debate about how to help the poor but affirmed her for the beautiful thing she had done and invested it with special significance (v. 8).

So often, the things we think we are doing for God are more about justifying ourselves to him and to other Christians. We think that everything we do should have a point. This woman simply came and poured out in a tangible way the love that was in her heart. Love was the point. And when she came a second time to anoint Jesus' body for burial after the crucifixion, she was too late! He had risen (Mark 16:1–6).

# Prayer

*Take my love; my Lord, I pour*
*At Thy feet its treasure-store:*
*Take myself, and I will be*
*Ever, only, all for Thee!*

# The Way We Live

# Trumpets and tiaras

'Everything they do is done for others to see.'
MATTHEW 23:5

It may not have caught your attention, but a while ago an awards ceremony was cancelled. Organized by a Christian radio station, the event was due to be held at the Savoy Hotel. The station asked its 500,000 listeners to nominate celebrities and public figures who 'embodied Christian ideals'. There was a good response and the organizers whittled down the nominees to a final list of twelve personalities.

The individuals were contacted, informed of their nomination and invited to the splendid bash where they would be duly awarded. But eight declined and four didn't even bother to reply. The station refused to blow the whistle on its reluctant nominees, but hinted that a top ten pop star and a premiership footballer were on the list.

The organizers were less than happy at having to cancel their plans and suggested that these high-profile celebrities were somehow ashamed of their beliefs, but I am not so sure that was the case. Perhaps they were sending another message about a decidedly tacky idea. After all, there are enough plastic awards ceremonies, so why add another to the list? There are too many unsung heroes and heroines across the UK who raise funds for good causes, serve their community selflessly, overcome personal difficulties with great courage and generally make life better for others.

Perhaps our shy celebs simply felt that when it came to embodying Christian ideals, there were some better examples to choose from. There may be another clue as well. One of the most neglected virtues of the faith is humility, and it could just be that some of those who were approached believed that attending such a ceremony would, in itself, demonstrate the opposite of a Christian ideal.

There is a famous story told of Groucho Marx, who belonged to the exclusive Friar's Club in Hollywood. He sent the secretary a telegram stating, 'Please accept my resignation. I don't want to belong to any club that will accept me as a member.'

It seems that there are others who feel the same way and would rather get on with their lives, quietly living out their faith as best they can. Personally, I found their rejection of trumpets and tiaras wonderfully refreshing.

The best awards and rewards are yet to come.

## For further reading

MATTHEW 23:1–12; LUKE 22:24–30

It wasn't only the Pharisees who were obsessed with status. Even at the last supper, the disciples were still arguing about which of them was the greatest. And if we're honest, can we say we are any different? We'd rather be recognized than overlooked. We prefer to have the best seats and it's pleasing to be admired and appreciated. But the Saviour who came to serve calls us to be part of his kingdom, where the greatest people are doing the serving, not sitting at the table (Luke 22:26–27). Even then, the temptation is to make sure people are watching us and seeing what great servants we are!

What does it mean, though, to be admired by people who are as sinful and fallible as we are? The only one who really counts is God: 'Then your Father, who sees what is done in secret, will reward you' (Matthew 6:6). The real test of our willingness to be servants is when we and God are the only ones who know what we have done.

## Prayer

*When it comes to service, there's usually a line that we draw about how far we're prepared to go. Ask God if he wants you to step over that line today.*

# Responsibility and blame

Do everything without complaining or arguing, so that you may become blameless and pure, children of God without fault in a crooked and depraved generation.

PHILIPPIANS 2:14–15

America must be a lawyers' paradise. Two legal stories illustrate the point. The first concerns a New York teacher who recently filed a lawsuit against a pupil for smoking in the lavatory. The aggrieved teacher claimed compensation for the cost of a doctor's visit plus damages for pain and suffering. He alleged that the cloud of smoke emerging from the cubicle gave him a sore throat, watering eyes and a headache.

A Pennsylvanian judge (thankfully) threw out the second. The potential defendant was God, being prosecuted by a man who claimed that the Almighty had failed to answer his prayers. The plaintiff said he had asked God for the gift of youth and the ability to play the guitar. Oh yes, and he also asked for his mother and pet pigeon to be raised from the dead. He argued that if God failed to appear in court, he should lose the case by default. The judge dismissed the suit as 'frivolous'.

Now before we get all smug and declare, 'It could never happen here', think again. We live in a complaint culture when at the drop of almost anything we are encouraged to stand by our rights. Whatever goes wrong, someone somewhere should take the blame.

I am all for citizens' charters but it seems to me that the writing on most of them is only down one side of the page. The balance comes when we make the parallel list headed 'Responsibilities'.

Here's a sample of what the other side of the page could look like:

1.  I promise not to lose my cool when something goes wrong, because that's the way it is sometimes.
2.  I promise to understand that most people who serve me do genuinely try to do the best they can most of the time.
3.  I promise that next time I screw up, I'll be honest and admit it.
4.  I promise to try and do to others as I expect them to do to me.
5.  I promise that when the buck is meant to stop with me, I'll let it.
6.  I promise that as long as I keep needing forgiveness, I'll keep giving it out.

Sorry if this sounds bad news for lawyers, but I have a feeling it may be better news for society.

## For further reading

Exodus 21

This passage in Exodus talks more about responsibilities than 'rights'. After the high drama of the giving of the Ten Commandments, these laws may seem a bit dry, especially because, at first sight, there are a lot that don't seem to apply to our lives today. A closer look, however, allows us to draw out of them ways in which God wants us to take responsibility for our actions. If we are in a position of authority or have the power to affect the lives of others, we should watch that we are fair and just (vv. 2–11). Our actions have consequences and we should be prepared to pay the penalty if we knowingly do wrong (vv. 12–32). Even if we have no intention of causing someone else harm or loss, but it occurs through our carelessness, we should face up to the consequences (vv. 33–34).

For the Israelites, the blessing that came to them through being God's special people gave them a duty to live in a different way from the people around them. We, who have received God's undeserved mercy and blessing, should be prepared to face up to our own responsibilities and act mercifully towards others.

## Prayer

*Teach me, Lord, to think before I act or speak, and always to remember that I have received from you what I could not earn and do not deserve. Help me to act towards others as you have acted towards me.*

# Rules to live by

Do not be wise in your own eyes; fear the Lord and shun evil.

PROVERBS 3:7

Just imagine you were asked to pass on the benefits of your wisdom (or lack of it) to a bunch of teenage school leavers.

When Bill Gates, founder of the Microsoft empire, was invited to a speech day at a California high school, he offered the following pearls of wisdom under the heading '11 Rules for Life'.

1. Life is not fair; get used to it.
2. The world won't care about your self-esteem. The world will expect you to accomplish something before you feel good about yourself.
3. You will not make $40,000 a year straight out of school. You won't be a company director with a car phone until you earn both.
4. If you think your teacher is tough, wait till you get a boss.
5. Flipping burgers is not beneath your dignity. Your grandparents had a different word for it—opportunity.
6. If you mess up, it's not your parents' fault. So don't whine about your mistakes; learn from them.
7. Before you were born, your parents weren't as boring as they are now. They got that way from paying your bills, cleaning your clothes and listening to you talk about how cool you are.
8. Your school may have done away with winners and losers, but life has not. In some schools, they have abolished failing grades and they will give you as many chances as you want to get the right answer. This does not bear the slightest resemblance to anything in real life.

9. Life is not divided into terms. You don't get summers off and very few employers are interested in helping you 'find yourself'. Do that on your own time.
10. Television is not real life. In real life, people actually have to leave the coffee shop and go to work.
11. Be nice to nerds. Chances are, you'll end up working for one.

I would add a twelfth rule to the list and place it right at the top. It is not particularly cool or politically correct but it offers advice that has stood the test of time, and in a society that offers us so much to live with and so little to live for, these are words worth heeding: 'Remember your Creator in the days of your youth' (Ecclesiastes 12:1).

## For further reading

PROVERBS 3

The upshot of Bill Gates' '11 Rules for Life' is that life is probably going to be tougher than you think, and that the world is an unforgiving, intolerant place. Lists of rules for more effective living and self-help books, with their pithy advice and helpful sayings, are all the rage. It's hard to resist them and not to take on board their often helpful, sometimes unhelpful advice on how to live a better, happier, more productive life. But it's important that we filter the wisdom of the world through God's word, both by knowing well what the Bible says and by testing what other people say against it. Perhaps the book of Proverbs could be described as the first 'self-help manual', the gathering together of godly sayings and wisdom in one place. Unlike most of today's books, Proverbs focuses not on 'me' but on seeking God's wisdom and putting him first.

## Prayer

*'To the only wise God be glory forever through Jesus Christ! Amen'* *(Romans 16:27).*

# Recognition

'But when you give to the needy, do not let your left hand know
what your right hand is doing, so that your giving may be in secret.
Then your Father, who sees what is done in secret, will reward you.'

MATTHEW 6:3–4

Gwyneth Paltrow's name and face are rarely out of the news. Her
sparkling talent as an actor creates an intense interest in her private life,
which means that she is one of those instantly recognizable people,
especially in her home country, the US of A.

But not everyone recognizes the recognizable. Some years ago,
Gwyneth Paltrow attempted to hail a taxi during the New York rush
hour but all the cabs were taken. She decided to risk recognition and
jumped on a subway train, no doubt hoping that if anyone did spot her,
they wouldn't make too much fuss.

In her carriage was a woman who was partially disabled, and they
got into conversation. They travelled to the same station and Paltrow
helped her on to the platform. There was a large escalator, so she
accompanied the woman and her luggage to street level.

Having played her walk-on good Samaritan part, Gwyneth bent
forward and hugged the stranger. The elderly woman fished in her
handbag, pulled out a $5 bill and said, 'This is for you. Get yourself
some food, dear. You look as if you could do with a good meal!'

To this particular traveller, the pencil-thin, glamorous Hollywood star
was just some poor underfed student who wasn't eating properly.

During the Advent season, we witness many hundreds of carol
services across the country. Among the carefully chosen Bible readings,
the first chapter of John's Gospel will no doubt be included in many
services. Here are some familiar words from a contemporary

paraphrase: '[Jesus] was in the world, the world was there through him, and yet the world didn't even notice' (John 1:10, *THE MESSAGE*).

There is something amusing and quite touching about the elderly woman failing to spot the star. But failing to notice the author of life itself is a different ball game. We hear the story of our down-to-earth God retold and wonder how people could miss the obvious, yet we run the risk of making the same mistake.

Christmas *is* a good time to party, renew friendships, give gifts, share food and celebrate life. A 'Bah humbug!' world that outlaws laughter and regards anything remotely approaching fun with grave suspicion is a long way from the Maker's intention—as long as we don't fail to recognize the recognizable.

## For further reading

3 JOHN:1–13

Some people work hard for recognition; politicians usually have one eye on how history will regard them; fame can be a consuming ambition. Most of us know that our name won't ever make the headlines but appreciation is quite a different matter. Two very different men make their appearance in John's third letter: Diotrophes, 'who loves to be first' (v. 9), and Gaius, to whom the letter is addressed. Even though John was planning a visit (vv. 13–14), he still went to the trouble of writing this letter of appreciation and encouragement to Gaius, who was putting his faith into practice in difficult conditions. Demetrius was commended as well (v. 12).

A little encouragement goes a long way. The absence of any recognition of our efforts can be demoralizing, and to have our motives misunderstood or misrepresented can be devastating. There are times when this will happen and then we can take encouragement from knowing that God 'sees what is done in secret' (Matthew 6:4), and that pleasing him brings the best reward.

## Prayer

*Lord, I want to bring glory to you by the way I live my life. Grant me the humility to put others first and to persevere even when my efforts are unappreciated by anyone but you.*

# Putting your foot in it

I consider [everything] rubbish, that I may gain Christ and be found in him, not having a righteousness of my own that comes from the law, but that which is through faith in Christ—the righteousness that comes from God and is by faith.

Philippians 3:8–9

If you have put your foot in it this week, here's a story to cheer you up.

Sir Thomas Beecham, the famous conductor, was walking into the foyer of a Manchester hotel when he spotted a distinguished-looking woman who recognized him and offered a smile. He remembered that he knew her from somewhere, but couldn't place who she was. He stopped and held one of those wonderfully polite British conversations, hoping that the woman would give away some clue to her identity.

During the conversation, Beecham recalled that the woman had a brother and that somehow their connection was through him. So he launched into a line of enquiry, hoping that this would reveal the woman's identity. 'Your brother, is he well?' Beecham asked. On hearing that he was in fine form, he probed further. 'And what's he doing with himself these days?' he enquired. 'Oh, he's still the king,' the woman replied.

I was reminded of the story when I read of two glider pilots in Scotland who began to lose altitude. They spotted a 'nice-looking field' close to the River Dee and decided to put down. On doing so, they found themselves surrounded by armed police officers.

It turned out that the field was the cricket lawn at Balmoral, and the whole incident had been watched by the Queen and other members of the royal family, who were taking afternoon tea. Far from being alarmed or annoyed, Her Majesty was concerned to know if both pilots were unharmed.

Many of us feel that to put your foot in it is one thing, but to offend royalty is somehow even worse. I am convinced that the same feeling exists when it comes to approaching God. An awkward mixture of embarrassment and fear of getting our words wrong combines with our personal feelings of guilt and inadequacy.

By contrast, the Bible paints a picture of a down-to-earth God who doesn't stand on ceremony in the person of Jesus Christ. It is not correct protocol that interests him but honest, open, humble people who come with all their doubts and failures hanging out.

That is what lies at the heart of this important statement: 'The church is not made up of people who are better than the rest, but of people who want to become better than they are.'

## For further reading

MATTHEW 23:27–39

It is possible to be very insular in our churches, saying the right things, being orthodox, subduing our doubts and postponing our questions. But it is only when we are prepared to admit to doubts and failures, to not having the answers to all of life's questions, that our faith can be demonstrated to be real. We have faith despite not knowing it all, despite our failures to live truly godly lives, despite our unanswered prayers, because our faith is in God and not in our own knowledge, abilities or success. Surely, the faith of a person who gets things wrong, who doesn't always win a victory over discouragement, who sometimes needs to say sorry and does it, is more persuasive to those outside the church than a Christian 'clone' who always smiles, has an answer for everything and doesn't seem to live in the same world as they do. The challenge to us is to live risky lives in which we might be exposed for who we really are, because it is Christ's righteousness that we are dependent on, not our own.

## Prayer

*Lord, thank you that my salvation does not depend on me but on Jesus' perfect life and obedient death. May I live before others honestly so that I do not mislead them into thinking that only perfect people are acceptable to you.*

# 'Mingle with the crowd' days

But you are a chosen people, a royal priesthood, a holy nation, a
people belonging to God, that you may declare the praises of him
who called you out of darkness into his wonderful light.

1 PETER 2:9

When Sir David McNee was Metropolitan Police Commissioner, he told
a story that reflected the increased complexities of policing.

A group of policemen who were sitting a promotion exam faced this
question:

*You are patrolling a shopping centre when there is an explosion. A man shouts
that his gas cooker is in flames and his wife, who is pregnant, has gone into
labour on the kitchen floor. As a result of the explosion, two cars travelling in
opposite directions have collided, blocking the main road. One is driven by a
woman you recognize as your Chief Superintendent's wife. You notice that she
smells strongly of alcohol and her tax disc is out of date. The other driver fits
a description circulated earlier of a man wanted concerning recent raids on
building societies. You notice that a case on the back seat of his car has burst
open and bank notes are spilling from it. As you are taking stock of the
situation, a distressed woman informs you that her dog, frightened by the
crash, has bolted, knocking a child into the canal at the rear of the shops. She
can't swim and the child is drowning.*

The exam question concluded, 'State what action you would take and
the order in which you would take it.'

McNee reported that the officer who came top simply wrote on his
paper, 'Remove uniform and mingle with crowd.'

I often think of that story on days when I'm tempted to throw in the towel. It may be apocryphal but it makes an important point. Sometimes it is an attractive option simply to walk away and pretend that, whatever the problem, it has nothing to do with me.

At times, I find being a Christian downright embarrassing and the activities (or inactivities) of the Church a travesty of the gospel we are meant to believe. I can sympathize with those who claim to have found God and left the Church. It even sounds attractive, until I realize that it is no more than self-indulgent escapism.

To run away from problems is to admit to our own inability to make a difference. Used creatively, frustration can be a powerful impetus for positive change.

On 'remove uniform and mingle with the crowd' days, I recall Jesus' words: 'You did not choose me, but I chose you' (John 15:16). Real discipleship, you see, is not based on my choosing but on God's calling.

## For further reading

1 PETER 2:9–25

In his letter, Peter is addressing the temptation to give up and blend in with the crowd in the face of criticism. The Christians he was writing to may have wondered what was the point of trying to live good lives when they were going to be accused of doing wrong anyway (vv. 11–12). Peter counters this by holding up Jesus as an example of how to act when facing persecution: he didn't retaliate or threaten, because his mind was fixed on God and on pleasing him rather than defending himself (v. 23).

When people give us a hard time, they think that it is a matter between us and them; Peter wants us to regard it as a matter between God and us. God has called us to follow him and he is the one to whom we are answerable. Jesus did not seek to justify himself to the fickle, fallible people around him but to his heavenly Father, the one 'who judges justly' (v. 23). When we are called upon to stand out from the crowd, it may bring criticism or slander down upon us, but it is not to the crowd that we are accountable. We are free to choose to live holy lives, determined by our desire to please God and not by how other people treat us (v. 16).

## Prayer

*May the way I act not be determined by the way other people treat me but only by my desire to please you, Lord of my life and my salvation.*

# Mind your language

'But I tell you: Love your enemies and pray for those who
persecute you, that you may be sons of your Father in heaven.'
MATTHEW 5:44

Mocking religion is bad for business, according to a report published a
number of years ago by the Advertising Standards Authority.

Detailing public complaints about the use of religious images to sell
products from jeans to lager, the Authority pointed to the results of a
recent survey, which showed that 78 per cent of those interviewed
believed disrespectful references to any religion should never be allowed.

A spokesman for the Authority said, 'Advertisers need to strike a
balance between creativity and sensitivity. Using religious references
can cause offence, especially if presented in a way that could be seen as
disrespectful or mocking.'

I believe we need to go further, without becoming poker-faced or
bland. How about an end to the frequent use of 'religious' swearing,
particularly on the broadcasting networks? My son switched on the car
radio the other day and tuned in to Radio 1. Within a couple of minutes,
the presenter let fly with a 'Christ Almighty' as he introduced an item,
as though it was nothing more than a slick link between sentences.

Recent years have seen advances on the discrimination front, many
of them sorely needed. Racial bigotry is fuelled by unchecked language.
It is about time our blasphemy laws received a long overdue revision as
well. I agree that the stuffiness of some aspects of religious behaviour is
fair game for humour, but the diet of blasphemy that comes through TV
and radio every day could and should be stopped.

If the Radio 1 presenter had used the name of Mohammed or
Buddha last week, I suspect there would have been a reprimand. There

is often greater sensitivity to the feelings of religious minorities, for understandable reasons. But all faiths need equal protection under law and it is about time the law was changed to provide it.

I have a friend who played squash at a fairly high level. He had an interesting technique when an opponent missed a shot and let out a curse such as 'Jesus Christ'. He used to look them straight in the eye and say, 'What has he got to do with it? If you are such a naff player, blame yourself, not him.'

We need similar straight talking across the wider population. We don't have to put up with offensive language or images, whether from advertisements or broadcasters. The mark of a society's maturity is seen not in what it permits, but in what it protects.

## For further reading

2 KINGS 2:15–25

Elisha, God's prophet, had been well-received and treated with courtesy in Jericho, but on the road to Bethel, a centre of Baal worship, it was quite different. He must have felt very vulnerable when a gang of youths came out of the town and began to mock him. Perhaps he felt physically threatened as well as upset by their insulting manner. As God's representative, he 'called down a curse on them in the name of the Lord' (v. 24), but he may have been as surprised as the youths were when the bears suddenly appeared and attacked them.

It is natural to want to retaliate when we are ridiculed or threatened, and it's tempting to think that people who have harmed us have got what they deserve when they suffer in some way. But we are called to do what does not come naturally or easily: Jesus said, 'Love your enemies and pray for those who persecute you' (Matthew 5:44). We don't have to stay silent when people are offensive about our faith, but we are called to love them as well.

## Prayer

*Call to mind someone in the public eye who appears to live a life that mocks God, and pray that he would reveal to them how much he cares for them.*

# Making the world a better place

**If we claim to be without sin, we deceive ourselves and the truth is not in us.**
1 JOHN 1:8

They say that confession is good for the soul, so here goes.

A while ago, a publisher wrote enclosing a manuscript. They wanted a cover endorsement for a new book and, to complicate matters, the author happened to be a friend of mine.

I found some time and a quiet place to read, and I was thrilled. It was a good book—no, it was a brilliant book and one that was worthy of record sales. I was pleasantly stunned.

And that is when it happened—quiet, unexpected, vicious. A bright, sunny afternoon went dark for a few short minutes as I was gripped by more than enthusiasm.

Jealousy in its festering form grabbed me by the throat. It throttled me slowly with a list of 'what ifs?' This book could be a bestseller; the author would make money, achieve fame and perhaps be nominated for a prestigious award. I felt overwhelmed with each sickening possibility. But all was not lost: I could refuse to give an endorsement or, better still, let loose the damning arrows of faint praise.

Talk about 'lead us not into temptation'. I was wallowing in the sticky sludge and in danger of drowning.

OK, so I didn't drown, but it was close. I wrote a rave review, but it hurt. It so happens that I met the author a day or so later, and it was then that I felt the surge of relief at having done the right thing. I congratulated him and meant it. I basked in his appreciation and offered best wishes on the book launch before walking away with a clear conscience and a light step.

I am not applying for sainthood—I lose too many battles for that. But I offer my tiny victory as a picture that illustrates a statement from the world's most famous sermon. Jesus said, 'Give to the one who asks you, and do not turn away from the one who wants to borrow from you' (Matthew 5:42).

Giving may not involve money. Thanks, appreciation, encouragement, time, friendship and laughter all qualify—oh yes, and book endorsements, even when giving them hurts! Whenever I am tempted to do something negative but choose instead to do something positive, I become a giver. And givers always make the world a better place.

## For further reading

GALATIANS 6:1–10

We are all sinful and would probably admit it, but the danger comes when we imagine that there are some sins we would never be tempted to commit. When we see someone else sinning in a way that we think we would never do, our first reaction might well be to condemn rather than to 'restore that person gently' (v. 1) or support those who are burdened with particular weaknesses (v. 2). We need each other, because no one is exempt from temptation. It is easier to resist it if we know that our Christian friends will call us to account for our actions.

Paul makes it very plain that we need to be clear in our minds about the truth: pleasing our sinful nature may bring short-term gratification but it leads to eventual 'destruction', whereas living to please the Spirit will bring blessing in the end if we persevere (vv. 8–9).

## Prayer

*Heavenly Father, every day I am faced with the choice of whether to please you or whether to please myself. All too often, pleasing myself looks so much more attractive. At other times, I don't even think about the choice I am making. Give me good friends who will challenge me when I sin, and help me to be clear in my mind that a life lived to please you is the only kind of life worth living.*

# The marshmallow test

'Do not be afraid. Stand firm and you will see the deliverance the
Lord will bring you today.'
EXODUS 14:13

When was the last time you had your EQ checked? Like me, you
probably wouldn't know where to find it, let alone have it assessed. The
initials were coined in a book written by Daniel Goleman, a science
correspondent with the *New York Times*. We are familiar with the
abbreviation IQ, meaning the way in which someone's intelligence is
measured. EQ is the same idea, but it deals with emotional intelligence
—in layman's terms, how you cope under pressure. Goleman's main
idea is that assessing someone's IQ may be less important than
discovering their character. His goal is to redefine what it means to be
smart.

One research test involved tempting a group of four-year-olds with
marshmallows. The researcher invited the children, one by one, into a
plain room. On the table sat a marshmallow. 'You can have the sweet
now if you want,' the child was told, 'but if you wait while I run a short
errand, you can have two marshmallows when I return.' The researcher
then left and the child's responses were secretly filmed.

Some gave in at once and stuffed the sticky treat into their mouths;
others lasted for a couple of minutes. Some held out against the odds:
they covered their eyes, put their heads down, sang loudly, played
games and even fell asleep in order to gain a double prize from the
researcher.

Does it sound like some expensive fun to produce another report full
of psychobabble? Think again.

When these same children were re-examined in their teenage years, interviews with their parents and teachers revealed that those who had held out for the second marshmallow were generally better adjusted, more dependable, popular, confident and emotionally rounded. The 'grabbers', by contrast, were more likely to be lonely, stubborn and frustrated, with a greater tendency to back down from challenges and give up easily. When academic test scores were checked, the youngsters who could hold out on the marshmallow test were, on average, 210 points higher on the scale.

Educating minds without developing characters is leaving a job half done. C.S. Lewis once observed, 'Education without values, as useful as it is, seems rather to make man a more clever devil.'

Perhaps that is why the Bible emphasizes that God seems far more concerned with what we have become than with what we have achieved.

## For further reading

Exodus 14:10–31

There are probably times in your life that you can look back on and say, 'God did it. Against the odds, God worked out that situation in a way I could barely have hoped for or foreseen.' Perhaps a door that had been closed suddenly opened; an opportunity came along that hadn't seemed possible before; the most unlikely person became a Christian (you, perhaps!). Thank God that he is a God of miracles, to whom all things are possible (Mark 10:27).

The Israelites were panicking, caught between Pharaoh's mighty army and the sea (Exodus 14:10). Moses' rallying speech was very simple: 'Don't be afraid; don't run; watch what God will do to rescue us.' The first instruction was the most difficult; as for the other two, they didn't have much choice. And what a fantastic, impossible miracle they saw! From it they learned a lot about God's power, his uniqueness and his unfailing love.

We may be the kind of people who pass the marshmallow test with flying colours or we may not. God isn't concerned primarily with our achievements but with what we think of him.

## Prayer

*'Who among the gods is like you, O Lord? Who is like you—majestic in holiness, awesome in glory, working wonders?' (Exodus 15:11).*

# Keep your cool

'Whoever can be trusted with very little can also be trusted with much, and whoever is dishonest with very little will also be dishonest with much.'

LUKE 16:10

What helps you when you're stressed?

I guess most of us have found good ways to cool down when things hot up, but I confess to being astonished at one solution offered to those at odds with modern technology.

If mobile phones, with their annoying ring tones, make you hot under the collar, then help is at hand. The nation of Finland hosts the annual World Mobile Phone Throwing Championship, which is open to all who hate one of the most influential inventions of recent years.

The competition held its fourth event on the island of Riihisaari a while ago. It was divided into two sections: traditional mobile phone throwing and a freestyle event. The former was judged purely on the length of the throw, but the second category allowed points to be scored for creative run-up, style of throw and overall artistic skill.

The organizer claims that all kinds of people from different countries are drawn together, each sharing a common cause: all of them are boiling with frustration at the advent of the mobile phone.

The world record for distance (66.72 metres) was set by a Finn hurling a Nokia 5110. But the report didn't say whether the owner was still attached when the phone was thrown.

It makes me wonder if a whole new Olympic competition could be launched, with events covering pet hates: smashing a speed camera, tossing the parking meter and burning junk mail, perhaps.

Stress, as a term to describe physical and psychological wear and tear brought on by anxiety, has only been around for 50 years. It was coined by Hans Selye, a Canadian scientist who published an influential book on the subject in 1950. In his dedication of the weighty tome, he makes the following tribute: 'Most personally this book is dedicated to my wife, who helped me so much to write it for she understood that I could not and should not be cured of my stress, but merely taught to enjoy it.' Mrs Selye sounds like a wise woman.

Throwing a mobile phone as far as you can may help you to 'enjoy' stress, but there's something much less expensive and much more effective. Jesus said, 'Come to me, all you who are weary and burdened, and I will give you rest' (Matthew 11:28).

## For further reading

Daniel 3:13–30

How well do you keep cool when things hot up? When a major problem occurs, all the minor, everyday pressures of living seem to take a back seat, but it is the way we learn to handle the 'little' stresses that lays the foundation for handling the big ones.

For Shadrach, Meshach and Abednego, things were literally 'hotting up' but they faced their ordeal calmly, not seeking to make excuses, simply affirming their faith in the God who had proved faithful to them in the past when they had honoured him (Daniel 1:6–16). They knew that God was able to save their lives, but their faith went even deeper than that: they would not betray his trust even if he chose to work things out differently.

Compromising our beliefs, losing our temper, being oversensitive or feeling sorry for ourselves when things go wrong may seem of minor importance at the time, but if God is going to be able to trust us with harder challenges, then we need to win the easier battles first.

## Prayer

*Meditate on these verses from Psalm 31:*

*In you, O Lord, I have taken refuge;*
*let me never be put to shame;*
*deliver me in your righteousness.*
*Turn your ear to me,*
*come quickly to my rescue;*
*be my rock of refuge,*
*a strong fortress to save me.*
*Since you are my rock and my fortress,*
*for the sake of your name lead and guide me (vv. 1–3).*

# How to handle criticism

*Written in January 2001*

Those whom I love I rebuke and discipline. So be earnest, and repent.
REVELATION 3:19

The recent death of one of Britain's most distinguished lawyers, George Carman QC, has brought a stream of recollections and tributes.

By all accounts, his courtroom performances were something to be seen. He became a master of the soundbite and knew how to win a jury over with a well-researched and brilliantly presented case.

In one of his most memorable putdowns of a famous witness, he told the court that the man 'had behaved like an ostrich, and put his head in the sand, thereby exposing his thinking parts'.

I would imagine that being examined by Carman was an experience you were unlikely to forget and unwilling to repeat. But even if we don't face a dazzling QC in courtroom mode, most of us face relentless cross-examinations that come in other forms and can be just as painful. I read in a book a couple of days ago, 'If you are never criticized, then you can't be doing much.' It was a message I needed to hear that particular morning.

It seems to me that criticisms come in three basic groups. The first group is based on ignorance or simple misunderstandings, and these criticisms can usually be dealt with by explaining the facts. The second group are usually vindictive and downright nasty: no matter what you say or do, nothing will be right in the eyes of those lobbing their particular grenades. Experience suggests that you should put on your tin helmet and settle down in the trench for a spell.

The third group of criticisms are the valuable ones, even if they're sharp and angry. They often contain a nugget of truth that, if unpacked with care, can make me a wiser and better person.

Martin Luther expressed it well when he wrote, 'I had rather that true and faithful teachers should rebuke and condemn me and reprove my ways, than that hypocrites should flatter me and applaud me as a saint.'

I guess, when it comes to handling criticism, we share the same dilemma: knowing which ones to bin and which ones to heed.

Fortunately, in the long run there's no need to fear even the most dazzling QC. Just leave it to the Judge who even judges judges.

## For further reading

REVELATION 3:7–22

These are two of the seven letters to the churches in the book of Revelation. Each is tailored to a slightly different situation. In the first five, there are words of commendation as well as criticisms, but the letters to the churches in Philadelphia and Laodicea differ somewhat. The Philadelphian Christians have endured patiently despite having 'little strength' (vv. 8, 10) and receive praise and encouragement. The Laodiceans, on the other hand, are proud and self-sufficient (v. 17) and there is nothing to commend. Yet the harsh criticism of the Laodicean church is done in a context of love, not to condemn utterly but to bring about positive change (vv. 19–20).

Criticism is easier to receive if we know it is done not out of spite but so that we might do better. If we find ourselves in the position of giving rather than receiving criticism, we should bear this in mind. It is helpful to look at who is criticizing us when we assess how we should receive what is said. The 'wounds from a friend can be trusted' (Proverbs 27:6) but there is sometimes a grain of truth in the words of our enemies, and if we are humble we can learn even from that.

## Prayer

*Thank you, Father, for loving friends who are willing to take a risk and criticize me when I need it. Give me an ear to hear what you say to me through them.*

# Frisbees and converts

And what does the Lord require of you? To act justly and to love mercy and to walk humbly with your God.
MICAH 6:8

When a sun-kissed Bank Holiday weekend comes round, and you happen to find yourself in a picturesque rural beauty spot, you may be tempted to join in a spot of Frisbee-throwing with the youngsters. On the other hand, you may settle for that time-honoured sport of sitting in the sun and watching the world go by.

As the father of four sons, I have thrown and caught my fair share of Frisbees over the years. When packing the car for a holiday or day out, a Frisbee was as essential as a thermos flask. So I was fascinated a while ago to read the obituary of the man who made this toy a worldwide bestseller.

Ed Headrick was taken on by a company in the 1960s, having persuaded them that he was brimful of good ideas. He offered his services for three months without pay, simply to convince them that he was worth hiring. One of the first products he tackled was a little-known children's toy marketed by the company under the name 'Pluto Platter'—an attempt to cash in on the fascination with UFOs.

Headrick spotted that the product was capable of better things, so he set about a comprehensive redesign. He created a more aerodynamic version by adding concentric grooves to the disc, and generally re-packaged the product to give it a more adult and sporty image. The results were amazing: in the mid-60s the Frisbee (literally) took off. Since then, more than one hundred million have been sold and a cheap child's toy has evolved into a piece of all-age sporting equipment.

But how did the Frisbee get its name? A bunch of bored university students at Yale started tossing around empty pie tins produced by the Frisbie Baking Company. One of the students saw potential in the craze and sold a plastic version to the Wham-O Company, who, in turn, developed the children's toy. Then Ed Headrick came along.

The ability to see beyond what is, and transform it, is a special gift. Turning an empty pie tin into a Frisbee made money and fame. But changing a life for the better yields richer rewards.

The Bible calls it conversion—and there's a lot of it about.

## For further reading

EXODUS 2

Do you consider yourself successful? Or do you look back on missed opportunities and regret how things have turned out? How does God see your life? Compared to his fellow Israelites, Moses began with great advantages, not as one of the slaves (Exodus 1:11–14) but adopted into the royal family (2:10). His career did not build on that early promise, however, because he could not ignore the sufferings of his own people, and his anger at their treatment led him to commit murder (vv. 11–12). He went on the run and settled in Midian, a dry and desolate place, as 'an alien in a foreign land' (v. 22), and he stayed there for 40 years (Acts 7:30).

Moses must have thought that nothing would ever change, but that was not God's plan. Are you where God wants you to be right now or is he saying to you, as he did to Moses, 'So now, go. I am sending you…' (Exodus 3:10)? Whichever is the case, God is in the life-changing business; we are to '*walk* humbly' with him (Micah 6:8), not to stand still.

## Prayer

*If you believe that God is calling you to something new, thank him for his guidance and clear leading. If he is calling you to stay where you are, ask him to renew your commitment to serving him there.*

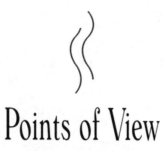

# Points of View

# Choices matter

*Written in July 2003*

'Those who do not carry their cross and follow me cannot be my disciples.'
LUKE 14:27

Laleh and Ladan Bijani spent 29 years sharing the same brain cavity and became the world's most celebrated Siamese twins. Their extraordinary situation meant that their two brains had fused together, causing enormous complications for surgeons who struggled to separate them in a marathon operation in Singapore.

The sisters were separated after 53 hours but, sadly, their condition was highly unstable and they died shortly afterwards. As the bodies were returned to their native Iran for burial, I listened to a moving interview with some of their family and friends. Inevitably, there were those who condemned the operation as foolhardy and pointed out that Laleh and Ladan had at least had some quality of life, despite their condition.

But it was a comment from the sisters' closest friend that struck me. They had known the risks that were involved and had made a conscious choice that they wanted to try for a better future.

Most of us would not be familiar with the name of Ed Roberts. In the mid-70s he created the world's first commercially successful personal computer (shortened to PC). He hired a 19-year-old called Bill Gates to write the software for him. Now there is a name that is instantly recognizable.

Roberts sold his computer business in 1977 and bought a farm. Seven years later, aged 41, he entered medical school. Today Bill Gates is a multi-millionaire and head of the largest software company in the world. Ed Roberts is a physician in a small town in Georgia, USA.

We may wonder if Roberts regrets his life-changing decision. After all, he could have made much more money and lived as a high-profile celebrity. But he has no doubts about his choice. Roberts says, 'The implication is that the PC is the most important thing I have ever done, and I don't think that is true. Every day I deal with things that are equally if not more important, here with my patients.'

Jesus drew a word-picture of two builders (Matthew 7:24–27). One opted for speed and built on sand; the other wisely chose a firmer foundation. When a storm broke, both buildings were tested to the limit. One stood and the other collapsed.

Choices matter.

## For further reading

Luke 14:25–33

We all make countless decisions in a lifetime, many of them with little forethought and without an awareness of the values that dictate them. Jesus says that we should give a lot of thought to the most important decision of all—whether to become his disciple—and weigh up the costs before we commit ourselves. If we are clear in our minds about what is important to us, it will be easier to make decisions when faced with a choice, and we need the firm foundation of faith in Christ when we experience the storms that result from making a costly but right choice.

Laleh and Ladan made the choice that was right for them after weighing up the risks. Ed Roberts does not feel, with hindsight, that the decision to sell his company and become a doctor was second-best. Sometimes it's worth asking ourselves, if I don't do this, will I regret it later on? If we make following Jesus our goal and think carefully and prayerfully about the decisions we need to make, we won't live to regret our choices.

## Prayer

*Have you made choices in the past that you have cause to regret? Ask God, who causes all things to work together 'for the good of those who love him' (Romans 8:28), to show you how he is doing that in your life.*

# It depends how you look at it

*Written in April 2003*

'Whether he is a sinner or not, I don't know. One thing I do know.
I was blind but now I see!'
JOHN 9:25

News coverage of the war in Iraq has brought few light moments, but the daily reports from one particular source have been a welcome exception.

Mohammed Saeed al-Sahaf, the Iraqi Information Minister, was in a league all of his own in his assessments of the progress of the war. Denials, accusations, gruesome descriptions and downright abuse were all included in his armoury of 'weapons of mouth destruction'.

We saw on TV pictures of coalition troops controlling the airport, but according to the minister they were running for their lives. As tanks rumbled into Baghdad, he steadfastly maintained that the invaders were being driven back. In a memorable piece of footage, a Marine was asked to comment on the Iraqi's claims, and the soldier answered, 'I think I'll pop across the road and let him know we are here.'

Now the man has become a legend and there is even a website in his name. It has been suggested that various railway companies, airports and banks could hire him as part of their customer service team. 'Madam, you only think you have a problem. The train is not late, it is standing at Platform 7. Trust me, I will take you and show you myself in just a minute.'

As the White Queen said to Alice in *Through the Looking Glass*, 'Why, sometimes I have believed as many as six impossible things before breakfast.'

This weekend, all across the world, millions will celebrate an impossible thing. Did the resurrection of Jesus of Nazareth really happen? Or are millions of believers as deluded as the Iraqi minister, spluttering out their absurd beliefs in the face of overwhelming facts?

I have reached my own decision based on the available evidence and I believe that it points to an empty grave. I don't believe the body was stolen, the disciples went to the wrong tomb, or that resurrection should be interpreted as a feeling rather than a fact. The simple statement of Paul (himself once an arch-opponent of the message of the resurrected carpenter) says it all: 'He was raised on the third day according to the Scriptures' (1 Corinthians 15:4).

Michael Ramsey, a former Archbishop of Canterbury, made a stark point: 'No resurrection, no Christianity.' And the amazing thing is this: there was, and there is.

## For further reading

JOHN 9:13–38

What a day this was! By the end of it, the man who had woken up blind every day of his life could see the physical world around him, and he had acknowledged that Jesus was the Son of Man. We hear him tell his story first to his neighbours and then, with mounting frustration, to the Pharisees, who become increasingly abusive.

The Pharisees' reasoning was that Jesus must be a sinner because he did not legalistically observe the religious rules that they kept, and since a sinner could not perform miracles, then the man couldn't have been blind in the first place (v. 18). The former beggar's reasoning was much simpler: 'Whether he is a sinner or not, I don't know. One thing I do know. I was blind but now I see!' (v. 25).

To know the truth about Jesus, we need to look beyond our own prejudices and be open to the evidence about him as it appears in the scriptures, in the testimony of those who have experienced him and in our own experience, and be willing to have our preconceived ideas challenged and possibly changed.

## Prayer

*Open my eyes, Lord, to see you as you truly are, not as I would like you to be. Give me a deep and simple faith in you, Son of God.*

# Come to me

'Come to me, all you who are weary and burdened,
and I will give you rest.'
MATTHEW 11:28

It is not often that Tintagel hits the headlines, but the national press recently carried news of a top award won by one of its residents.

The Best Business Name Award is presented by *Yellow Pages*, and Terry Melton from Tintagel won first prize. Terry's one-man gardening business trades as The Lawn Ranger and his ingenuity impressed the panel of judges so much that they gave him £1,000.

The runners-up displayed an equally ingenious turn of phrase: C-Air (an air conditioning firm), Jim'll Mix It (a cement specialist), Goochi Poochi (dog and cat groomers), You Can Never Have Too Many Shoes (a shoe shop), Petal Pushers (florists), Pride and Groom (another dog and cat groomer), Drips, Drains and Plumbing Pains (plumbers) and Wish You Wash Here (dry cleaners).

I think they should run a similar competition for churches, as there are some unusual titles around, including the Invisible Church (how you find it, I don't know). What impresses me about Terry Melton is that his title says exactly what he does—and perhaps that is a good starting point for churches too.

Some churches choose names from the Bible that are thought to be especially appropriate. So you find chapels called Ebenezer, which means 'The Lord has helped us', or Bethel, meaning 'The house of God'. Others pick the name of a saint, and some believe that the longer the title, the more important the church—for example, The Church of the Freeborn Redeemed Children of God whose Robes Have Been Washed in the Blood of the Lamb, Holy Spirit Prophecy Fellowship Incorporated. Hmmm.

My personal favourite comes from a new type of church. It's one of several initiatives springing up in various parts of the country as part of a bold movement to reach out to people who believe that institutional church has little to offer. They meet in a pub in a busy city centre and offer many of the things you would expect to find in a conventional church building. Singing, prayers, teaching, friendship and the opportunity to ask questions are all part of the staple menu offered in warm and friendly surroundings. I love their title: the church in the pub is simply called Bar None.

In the words of the advert, it does exactly what it says on the tin.

## For further reading

ISAIAH 57:14–21

Some people get the wrong idea about church if their experience of it has been limited or non-existent. Sadly, for others, their experience of church has given them the wrong idea about God, and instead of being drawn to him they have felt that their failings disqualify them from coming to church at all. Churches shouldn't be exclusive clubs for the initiated but communities that live out the invitation of Jesus to come, bring our burdens to him and exchange them for his rest (Matthew 11:28). The 'contrite and lowly in spirit' are always welcomed by God (Isaiah 57:15) but not always by churches.

We need to think about how to 'remove the obstacles' that deter people from coming (v. 14) and remind ourselves that everyone who walks past the door—and everyone who plucks up the courage to cross the threshhold—of our church is intimately known and loved by God, whoever they are and whatever they have done.

## Prayer

*Help me to play my part, Lord Jesus, in making my church a welcoming community that shows your love to those on the outside as much as to those who have already come in.*

# Through other people's eyes

The ways of the Lord are right; the righteous walk in them,
but the rebellious stumble in them.

HOSEA 14:9

One day, I was flicking through the *Western Morning News* in a hot and airless lounge, and I saw a picture from Pakistan of people cooling off in a river. The caption detailed the current heatwave, with temperatures hitting 125 degrees. Suddenly, I didn't feel quite so warm.

Then I read Mohammed Ismail's restrained comment after waiting since 1976 for the Bangladesh Telephone Board to connect him. (He finally has a line.) 'It was a frustrating experience. I needed the telephone very badly 27 years ago.' Suddenly, my frustration at losing my mobile signal for ten whole minutes seemed quite pathetic.

Then I heard of the appalling plight of Kaoru Hatakeyama, who has been in solitary confinement for 43 years in a Japanese prison. Forbidden to speak, the 80-year-old receives no visitors and is only let out for a bath or a few exercise periods in a cage measuring 6 by 15 feet. Suddenly, being 20 minutes late for an appointment because of a traffic jam wasn't so bad after all.

Seeing life through other people's eyes always restores perspective. So does refreshing our memories about personal struggles that we have come through. The old hymn reminds us to count our blessings, and that is wise advice.

A group of ten men who were lepers came to Jesus seeking a miracle. Leprosy is a terrible disease that scars and disfigures people emotionally as well as physically. These men were forced to live apart from their families and were considered outcasts by their communities. They lived at the bottom of the pile and relied on scraps of food and random acts of charity.

Remarkably, they received their healing and rushed off to get the medical certificates that would allow them to rebuild their broken lives, to sleep with their wives, to hug their kids, to share a meal with their parents. It must have been like starting life all over again.

One of them—just one—put the family celebrations on hold for a few minutes. 'When he saw he was healed, he came back, praising God in a loud voice. He threw himself at Jesus' feet and thanked him' (Luke 17:15–16).

Ten were healed but only one came back to say 'thank you'.

Ten to one. What are the odds on me living gratefully today?

## For further reading

HOSEA 1:1—2:1; 14:4–8

The gossips must have had a field day when Hosea married Gomer: 'Doesn't he know her reputation?' He certainly got everyone's attention for his message from God, as well as finding out for himself something of how God felt about Israel's unfaithfulness. When things started to go wrong in Hosea's marriage, did people say, 'I told you so'? And when Hosea took Gomer back into his home (3:1), did they feel resentful to see her getting better treatment than she deserved? Hosea's life illustrated plainly how God's people had treated God, how much he loved them and the extent of his willingness to forgive. Seeing things from God's point of view gave people the opportunity of a second chance if they chose to take it. Our lives are enriched and our attitudes can change when we open ourselves to look at things through other people's eyes. Is there something in your life that you need to ask God to give you a new perspective on?

## Prayer

*Teach me, Lord, more and more to see things from your perspective and to respond to other people as you would have me do.*

# The truth or a lie

*Written in November 2003*

Turn from evil and do good; seek peace and pursue it.
PSALM 34:14

A new phrase has entered our language, and many wish it hadn't—two words that stand innocent on a page, yet on a street mean blood, death, destruction, crippled bodies and disabled minds.

The 'suicide bomber' is the urban terrorist's deadliest weapon. This week the historic city of Istanbul has been rocked a second time by blasts aimed to create maximum damage and so generate maximum publicity.

Security experts suggest that no adequate protection exists against the suicide bomber, as those triggering the explosion are committed to die for their cause. Western minds, focused on self-preservation at all costs, find it hard to comprehend why a young person would go so far as to strap explosives to their body and willingly press a button blowing themselves to kingdom come. It's just a waste—and 'getting wasted', to an average Western 20-year-old, means something very different.

I mention 'kingdom come' deliberately, because that is the precise motivation that drives young people in the prime of life to surrender that life and sacrifice others into the bargain. Their belief, pure and simple, is that the death of a martyr in pursuit of a holy cause brings instant reward in the next life for the martyr and their immediate family. Allied to this promise of paradise, there is the offer of forgiveness of sins.

If you are a young person trapped in a refugee camp with little prospect of life improving, if you burn with indignation at what you see as gross injustice for your people, which has been ignored for years, then heaven on a plate is a huge temptation. To promote your cause, accelerate a solution, contribute to the ultimate victory and achieve your eternal security, it's an offer that many young men and women can't refuse.

Ideas have consequences. When we look at Auschwitz and ask, 'Why?' we only have to read *Mein Kampf* for the answer.

That is why people of goodwill who represent all faiths should affirm loud and clear that the promise of reward for martyrdom is a lie that creates false hope and promotes wanton violence. In the name of God, murder in God's name cannot be tolerated. 'Turn from evil and do good; seek peace and pursue it.'

## For further reading

ROMANS 1:16–32

Is it better to believe in something than in nothing at all? The suicide bomber has decided that there is nothing to live for now and has put his or her hope in a better future attained by a martyr's death. The people described in this passage (and perhaps we can think of more recent examples) have suppressed all thought of future consequences and are living for today, indulging their most basic appetites at every opportunity; they believe only in pleasing themselves. It's a slippery slope: one thing leads to another and their whole lives are corrupted (vv. 28–31).

If I am the ultimate truth in my life, if there is nothing and no one outside of me or greater than me, could there be anything more depressing? Is a mistaken belief-system that glorifies the indiscriminate murder of other people better or worse than that? Both display 'contempt for the riches of [God's] kindness, tolerance and patience' (Romans 2:4). We need to remind ourselves of the Saviour who died a lonely martyr's death on a cross to bring life, not death, to all who would believe in him.

## Prayer

*Lord, help me to seek you humbly, not judging others but acknowledging my own sin and need of you.*

# Does God have favourites?

'So the last will be first, and the first will be last.'
MATTHEW 20:16

Imagine your nine-year-old son coming home with a school report bearing this comment from the headmaster: 'Very bad, is a constant trouble to everybody and is always in some scrape or other. He cannot be trusted to behave himself anywhere. He has very good abilities.' Like any parent, you would try to scrape some crumb of comfort from the final remark but the rest of it makes depressing reading.

That report, issued by St George's School, Ascot, was dated 9 April 1884. And the young pupil, who must have prayed for his parents to forget to read it, was none other than Winston Leonard Spencer Churchill.

A second assessment of the same person was written 101 years later by Henry Kissinger, the distinguished former US Secretary of State:

*Our age finds it difficult to come to grips with the figures like Winston Churchill. The political leaders with whom we are familiar generally aspire to be superstars rather than heroes. The distinction is crucial. Superstars strive for approbation; heroes walk alone. Superstars crave consensus; heroes define themselves by the judgment of a future they see it as their task to bring about. Superstars seek success in a technique for eliciting support; heroes pursue success as the outgrowth of inner values.*

Two assessments of the same character; one written in the formative years of childhood, the other with the hindsight of history. Together they pose several questions.

First, are we guilty of interpreting people wrongly? The headmaster saw young Churchill as being always in trouble. But who can say whether his bulldog tenacity, which inspired a war-torn nation, was not fashioned in those years? Second, are we guilty of rejecting people who fail to fit a system? Some of the greatest movers and shakers in history were those who challenged the status quo. Third, are we guilty of reaching instant judgments about people? We all know 'it's not over till it's over', so why reach a hasty conclusion about a person's abilities before they have proved themselves? And the fourth question is possibly the most important: are we ourselves going to be blighted for life by one bad review, or will we rise above it and prove our critics wrong?

A word of encouragement for despairing parents and teachers: never put a book down when it's half read. The end is often much better than the beginning!

## For further reading

MATTHEW 20:1–16

Have you ever heard a sermon in which the preacher lists the spiritual credentials of himself, his wife, his children, even his grandchildren, with due expressions of humility, giving God all the glory? What about the person in the congregation who is really struggling because, however hard she prays and tries to set an example, her children are not glowing examples of Christian discipleship? What about the man with a failed marriage, lonely and in despair at times, who sits and smarts under such tactless preaching? Does God have favourites? Sometimes it seems like it.

This parable of Jesus is a timely warning to apparent favourites that God does not judge in the way we do, so we should serve him humbly and faithfully and not put our faith in outward appearances. Even more, it is an encouragement to the seemingly overlooked that the God we serve is 'generous' and there are going to be some surprises in the end.

## Prayer

*Pray whichever prayer applies to you.*

*Teach me, Lord, not to be boastful of your blessings as though in some way I deserve them. May the recognition of your goodness to me inspire me to serve you more faithfully.*

*Sometimes, Lord, I think you have forgotten me. Thank you for the encouragement in this parable that if I am patient you will use even me.*

# In Training

# Advice for running marathons

*Written in April 2004*

**Let us run with perseverance the race marked out for us. Let us fix our eyes on Jesus.**
HEBREWS 12:1b–2a


It's unusual for TV stars, politicians, top athletes and celebrity chefs to share a Sunday together—but not tomorrow.

The list of competitors for the London Marathon reveals that Iain Duncan-Smith and Jeffrey Archer will be joining Lorraine Kelly and Charlie Brooks to pound the streets of London. Gordon Ramsay will line up alongside Graham Gooch, while Michel Roux takes on Mark Hughes over the gruelling 26-mile course. Then there is the man I shall be looking out for—Fauja Singh, who is 93 years young and last year broke the world record for his age group by 45 minutes. He only took up running four years ago in order to keep fit.

A number of celebrities are planning to compete, but you may not spot them in the crowd of 46,000 runners. If you think that is a lot of people, it's around half of those who applied to take part. Interest in this world-famous race is so great that a ballot is held each year to decide who can run.

Since the first London Marathon in 1981, around half a million people have taken part, and tomorrow the West Country will be well represented in the big race that raises millions of pounds for good causes. I have several friends competing and recently I decided to support one of them on a training run around Burrator Reservoir. I managed eight miles and felt pretty pleased with myself, but that achievement was eclipsed by my schoolteacher friend (facing her first marathon), who clocked up an impressive 20 miles and looked none the worse for wear.

We bumped into some fellow runners who are competing this weekend in the Scilly Isles Marathon. The running fraternity are a friendly bunch so we swapped notes. They had one piece of veterans' advice for my friend. 'It's about two races,' they said. 'The first lasts 20 miles and is straightforward. The second is over six miles and is the killer. Hang in there and don't give up.'

They didn't realize it, but they gave me greater insight into a famous verse in the Bible that says, 'Let us run with perseverance the race marked out for us.'

So if the race is hard, don't give up. The finish is in sight.

## For further reading

PSALM 10:1–18

For Christians in some parts of the world, persecution is a part of daily life, but for many of us the Christian life is usually like jogging: we have to put ourselves out a little but it's not too strenuous. We don't experience life- or freedom-threatening persecutions and everyday life is fairly comfortable. But we can't count on it. Sometimes very dark times come. Ill health, bereavement, suffering for doing the right thing, financial reverses or failed relationships may bring us to the point of despair, and that's when we realize our need of God most clearly. It's wonderful to feel God's comforting presence and know his clear direction at times like that, but it's not always the case. Verse 1 of this psalm says, 'O Lord, why do you stand so far away? Why do you hide when I need you the most?' (Living Water).

When we are going through tough times and God seems far away, how should we react? By continuing to go through the motions, putting ourselves in the way of hearing from God again by reading the Bible, going to church and making time to pray. In verses 14 and 17 we are reassured that 'you, O God, do see trouble and grief; you consider it to take it in hand… You hear, O Lord, the desire of the afflicted; you encourage them and listen to their cry.' He hears and he will help. Don't give up; the end of the race is nearly in sight. Wait for him.

## Prayer

*If times are tough and you feel like giving up, pray, 'O Lord, why do you stand so far away? Why do you hide when I need you the most?' and expect God to answer.*

# A quiet place

'Come with me by yourselves to a quiet place and get some rest.'
MARK 6:31

My wife was invited to lead a seminar for health professionals, entitled 'Handling Stress'. 'That's interesting,' I said, 'but why did they choose you for that subject?' 'Because living with you has made me an expert,' was the reply.

Moving swiftly on, I heard two stress stories this week.

The first involves a busy husband flying around early in the morning, anxiously anticipating a major meeting he was due to attend. Running downstairs, briefcase in hand, he shouted a hasty goodbye. His wife popped out of the kitchen to see him off and was greeted by the sight of her immaculately turned-out man in his best suit, shirt and tie. He looked the part, except for one vital omission—his trousers.

The second concerns a harassed mum on the afternoon school run. Picking up her four children from their different schools, she fought her way through traffic. Arriving home, she settled one child for piano practice, the second for homework and the third to start making tea. The fourth had a dental appointment and she whisked him out of the door to do battle with the traffic again.

She made it with a minute to spare and ushered her son into the chair for his filling. The dentist peered into the boy's mouth and said, 'There's nothing wrong with his tooth.' The mother looked hard at her son for a moment and then exclaimed, 'Oh, no! I've brought the wrong one!'

Stress makes us do daft things because it scrambles our ability to think clearly. What can we do when it strikes?

Jesus knew what stress felt like and he knew how to handle it, too. An insight into his method comes in the Gospels, when his disciples were suffering from people pressure so greatly that they couldn't even find time to eat. Jesus took an executive decision and wrapped it up in a surprising invitation: 'Come with me by yourselves to a quiet place and get some rest.'

Jesus deliberately turned his back on the tyranny of the urgent in order to find the strength of renewal away from the crowds. 'I wish,' you might say. 'You can,' is my response. Here's a thought: if you want to give up something for Lent, try giving up noise.

## For further reading

MARK 6:30–46

The twelve disciples had been sent out by Jesus to preach and heal (6:12–13). Now reunited with him, they were eager to share all that they had experienced. With all the comings and goings around them, they hadn't even had a chance to eat, so Jesus' invitation to go off and be alone with him was very welcome.

We all need balance in our lives between the demands of other people and time to relax on our own or with those with whom we feel most comfortable, so it's easy to imagine the disciples' exasperation when, on arriving at the 'solitary place', they found that the crowd had arrived ahead of them. Jesus set them and us an example, however. He looked beyond the inconvenience to the need, and put himself out to meet it. And because the disciples didn't go off and sulk, they played a part in an amazing miracle: the feeding of the five thousand. Afterwards Jesus sent the disciples away ahead of the crowd, recognizing perhaps that they really had had enough by then, and finally went off himself 'up on a mountainside to pray' (v. 46).

## Prayer

*Thank you, Lord, that you know when we just can't cope with any more and you provide times of rest and refreshment for us. Help us to be wise in how we plan time off, but also help us to accept interruptions as opportunities from you so that we won't miss out on something better.*

# Less than the least

*Written in February 2003, in the week when Manchester United manager Sir Alex Ferguson
kicked a football boot that hit David Beckham*

Although I am less than the least of all God's people,
this grace was given to me: to preach to the Gentiles the
unsearchable riches of Christ, and to make plain to everyone
the administration of this mystery.

EPHESIANS 3:8–9

In a week when a football manager made the headlines by kicking a
boot rather than a ball, I came across a revealing interview with a less
fiery coach.

Sven-Goran Eriksson made headlines when he was appointed coach
of the England team because he was the first foreigner in the post. But
his quiet manner and thoughtful approach seem to have won him
respect.

When he got the job, he insisted that his longstanding friend, Tord
Grip, be made his number two in the England set-up. What I hadn't
realized was how deep and true that friendship ran.

About 30 years ago, the two played together for a small Swedish
team. In those days, the young Sven had dreams of becoming an international football star and landing a lucrative contract with an Italian
team. Grip was a wiser, older man who told his young friend bluntly
that he would never make the big time, at least as a player. A comment
like that could have spelt the end of their friendship.

Grip eventually finished playing and took a management position
with another club. He quickly hired Eriksson as his assistant and
encouraged him to develop his coaching skills. Eventually he left him

in charge of all training and tactics, and the club rose from Division 3 to 1 in successive seasons.

This success pushed Eriksson to international prominence, and he managed top clubs in Portugal and Italy before landing the prestigious England job. His blunt mentor, Tord Grip, has now become his assistant and seems happy to enjoy the benefits of his fulfilled prophecy.

Two things are underlined by this true and touching story—first, the benefit of talent spotters. How many people have ended up doing something really well, not because they thought they could do it but because someone else encouraged them along that path. It is a precious gift.

Second, the story reminds me of the value of true friendship. A real friend tells me what I need to hear rather than what I want to hear. True friends take risks by telling the truth. A genuine friend is the person who loves you enough to talk tough.

The Bible says, 'Wounds from a friend can be trusted' (Proverbs 27:6). (But that doesn't include those caused by flying football boots.)

## For further reading

ROMANS 12:1–8; 1 TIMOTHY 1:15–17

Paul encouraged the Christians in Rome to view themselves and their talents objectively (Romans 12:3), so it is revealing to look at how Paul saw himself. In Ephesians 3:8 he referred to himself as 'less than the least of all God's people', enabled by God's grace alone to exercise his powerful ministry. He even described himself to Timothy as 'the worst' of sinners (1 Timothy 1:15). Here we see Paul's continuing wonder at the God who showed 'unlimited patience' and 'mercy' to him (v. 16).

If we are ambitious to do something that we are not equipped for, it will end in disappointment. However, if we are prepared to look at ourselves honestly and listen to others, we will have the opportunity to be the best we can be. Sven-Goran Eriksson was humble enough to accept the assessment of his friend and became great doing something else as a result. As Christians, it should not be ourselves that we seek to exalt but the God who 'while we were still sinners' died in our place (Romans 5:8).

## Prayer

*Now to the King eternal, immortal, invisible, the only God, be honour and glory for ever and ever. Amen (1 Timothy 1:17).*

# What's the point?

I urge you to live a life worthy of the calling you have received.
EPHESIANS 4:1

A training seminar was organized for a government department. The theme of the study day was about resolving conflict between management and staff. Contributions from the floor were written on a flipchart. Someone suggested that a weakness in the department was the management's tendency to interfere on quite trivial issues. So the word 'nitpicking' was duly written on the flip chart. Suddenly one of the managers leapt to his feet. 'Shouldn't there be a hyphen between "nit" and "picking"?' he asked.

At the risk of being considered in the same mould, I want to raise the delicate issue of the long-life sandwich. (No pun intended.) In case you have been occupied with other pressing matters, let me bring you up to date.

The US military recently announced an astonishing discovery. They have created an 'indestructible sandwich' that stays fresh for up to three years and can withstand extreme heat, rough handling and air-drops. Available in two flavours (pepperoni and barbecue chicken), this breakthrough has been achieved following months of research by food scientists based in Massachusetts.

According to press reports, this discovery will enable greater efficiency within the military, as service personnel will no longer have to worry about stale or soggy sandwiches as they risk life and limb on the battlefield. Better still, we are told, this wonderful product will eventually make its way on to supermarket shelves, so we can all share in the scientific triumph.

Here comes the nitpicking part. How come so much time and effort are spent on things that, in the big plan, are not that important? If we could devote as much energy to eradicating world hunger, reducing the debt of countries in the developing world, tackling some of the basic health problems that afflict millions of children and working to provide every community with safe water supplies, I think we could live another century without the indestructible sandwich.

This morning I read a verse from the New Testament that simply says, 'You must not get tired of doing good' (2 Thessalonians 3:13, GNB). That provided a much-needed antidote to my cynicism and a reminder that there is a huge difference between actually doing good and simply being known as a 'do-gooder'.

It is easy to spend time and energy in the wrong direction. Surely we can offer a hungry, hurting world something more useful than an indestructible sandwich.

## For further reading

MATTHEW 23:1–24

If we are familiar with passages like this one, where Jesus castigates the Pharisees for their hypocrisy, we may fail to appreciate that when Jesus told people that their righteousness should exceed that of the Pharisees and teachers of the law (Matthew 5:20) they probably gasped and thought of giving up before they had even begun. The teachers were respected for adhering to the law that they studied with such devotion, and the Pharisees set themselves apart from 'sinners' and lived strictly according to their own rules and regulations, which went much further than the requirements of the law. They even tithed their herbs (23:23)!

The Pharisees and teachers had started off with admirable intentions but, along the way, external righteousness (how they looked to other people) had become more important than having hearts that were right with God. It reminds us that it is possible to get things right at the beginning but to go wrong in the end. Paul told the Corinthians, 'Examine yourselves to see whether you are in the faith; test yourselves' (2 Corinthians 13:5).

## Prayer

*Help me, Lord, to see the difference between the things that I do for you and the things that have become an end in themselves. Help me to change if I need to.*

# The Armour of God

Finally, be strong in the Lord and in his mighty power. Put on the full armour of God so that you can take your stand against the devil's schemes. For our struggle is not against flesh and blood, but against the rulers, against the authorities, against the powers of this dark world and against the spiritual forces of evil in the heavenly realms. Therefore put on the full armour of God, so that when the day of evil comes, you may be able to stand your ground, and after you have done everything, to stand. Stand firm then, with the belt of truth buckled round your waist, with the breastplate of righteousness in place, and with your feet fitted with the readiness that comes from the gospel of peace. In addition to all this, take up the shield of faith, with which you can extinguish all the flaming arrows of the evil one. Take the helmet of salvation and the sword of the Spirit, which is the word of God. And pray in the Spirit on all occasions with all kinds of prayers and requests. With this in mind, be alert and always keep on praying for all the saints.

EPHESIANS 6:10–18

# Stand your ground

*Written during the 2002 Winter Olympics*

Therefore put on the full armour of God, so that when the day of evil comes, you may be able to stand your ground, and after you have done everything, to stand.

EPHESIANS 6:13

'From Worst to First' is not a headline that most people would like to see written about themselves, but it's one that Steven Bradbury is more than happy with.

He has gone down in history as the first Australian gold medallist in the Winter Olympics. The extraordinary TV pictures of Bradbury's surprise win have gone around the globe. They showed him trailing the field in the skating final of the 1000-metre short track sprint, before a pile-up sent the leaders flying in all directions, leaving the rink scattered with bodies and the road clear for Bradbury to skate over the line into the gold medal position.

What makes his victory all the more remarkable is that no one expected him even to make the final. He escaped elimination in the quarter-finals because another skater was disqualified, and only made it through the semi-finals because of a crash on the ice.

The 'worst to first' headline came from the official Games news service but no one, it seems, begrudges Steve his win. All seemed genuinely pleased that the man who had no hope of a medal walked away with the gold.

People have already picked up the close similarities between Steve's story and the fable of the tortoise and the hare. It also illustrates a verse in the Bible that says, 'The race is not to the swift or the battle to the strong, nor does food come to the wise or wealth to the brilliant or favour to the learned; but time and chance happen to them all' (Ecclesiastes 9:11).

As uncomfortable as it may sound, the Bible says that we can't guarantee success. None of us can control the future or ensure that what we plan will happen. That doesn't mean we should live without aims, or work without dedication. Rather, we should remember that we don't own our lives but hold them on trust.

There is someone who sees and directs the big picture—and faith, in part at least, is about putting my plans under his ultimate control. Some call it escapism, but in fact it is realism. Once you recognize that you don't hold all the cards or possess all the answers, you get things into proper perspective and open the way for some amazing possibilities.

If you don't believe me, ask Steve Bradbury. He's got a medal to prove it!

## For further reading

EPHESIANS 6:10–18

As Christians, we are involved in a battle against much more than our own limitations. In this passage, Paul warns us that we are in a struggle not only against the evil we can see but against the unseen forces that direct and influence human affairs for evil (v. 12). Of course, this doesn't mean that we shouldn't fight against evil when we come across it, but Paul doesn't want us to underestimate our enemy. The first chapter of the book of Job demonstrates that the things we might put down merely to natural disaster or human wickedness may originate elsewhere. That's why we need to 'be alert and always keep on praying' for ourselves and each other (v. 18). We need 'the full armour of God', not a pick and mix selection of it. With it we will be able to withstand the devil's attacks, whether he comes as 'a roaring lion looking for someone to devour' (1 Peter 5:8) or masquerading 'as an angel of light' (2 Corinthians 11:14).

## Prayer

*Thank you. Father, that when I put on your armour I am not trusting in my own small strength but in your mighty power. Not only that, I am facing an enemy whom you have already defeated. Enable me to stand firm, I pray.*

# The belt of truth

*Written in February 2004*

Jesus answered, 'I am the way and the truth and the life. No one
comes to the Father except through me.'

JOHN 14:6

There have been some sermons from strange places this week.

The publication of the long-awaited report on the Hutton enquiry
into the death of Dr David Kelly has led to statements, interviews,
leaders, articles and studio debates. And the sermon topics are as varied
as they are numerous: the freedom of the press, the nature of truth,
personal integrity, the need for accuracy and the weight of personal
responsibility—a remarkable list.

I have found the whole thing fascinating and, strange as it may seem,
wonderfully reassuring. I intend to leave the sermonizing to others and
instead offer a list of reasons to be grateful.

I am glad to live in a democracy where government can be challenged
and questioned. I am also pleased we have a judicial system that is
thorough and basically honest. I am happy that a man's death is not
dismissed and that his memory is treated with dignity.

I think it is good that a captain of a team takes responsibility for
mistakes and resigns with good grace and maximum speed. I think it is
healthy that a public broadcaster can hold its hands up and say it got
something wrong.

I am grateful that we are grown-up enough to debate, argue and (we
hope) learn about the respective roles and responsibilities of government, the media and the public at large. These are good things that
make for a healthy society and, personally, I see them as a cluster of

God-given gifts 'coming down from the Father of the heavenly lights' (James 1:17).

When Mark Twain learned his trade as a journalist, he was taught the golden rule never to report anything as fact that he could not personally verify—the very issue that lies at the heart of Hutton.

Twain followed this instruction to the letter and wrote an account of a gala social event: 'A woman giving the name of Mrs James Jones, who is reported to be one of the society leaders of the city, is said to have given what purported to be a party yesterday to a number of alleged ladies. The hostess claims to be the wife of a reputed attorney.'

How boring to have a press that is gagged; how terrifying to have one that is unrestrained. How encouraging to live in a society where, most of the time, we know and prize the difference.

## For further reading

ACTS 4:13–20

Why did Paul illustrate the place of truth in the Christian's armour as a belt? A belt doesn't seem that important, as it doesn't protect against injury and cannot be used as a weapon. In fact, though, the soldier's belt was foundational in keeping the rest of the armour in place and ensuring that the armour functioned efficiently.

Jesus referred to himself as 'the truth', saying that he was the only way to God the Father, and this is the foundation of the message that we are called on to declare. It probably won't make us popular, but, if we are certain of the truth, we will go into battle boldly and use the weapons at our disposal effectively. At the last supper, Jesus had told his disciples that the Holy Spirit would reveal the truth to them (John 16:13), and in the passage in Acts 4 we see the result of this, as Peter and John refuse to give up speaking about Jesus: 'For we cannot help speaking about what we have seen and heard' (v. 20). They knew the truth and they couldn't keep quiet about him.

## Prayer

*Jesus, there are lots of people who would like to say that you are just one of many ways to come to God, and it isn't fashionable or popular to say that you are the only way. I affirm again that you are 'the way and the truth and the life' and I thank you for revealing yourself to me.*

# The breastplate of righteousness

*Written in January 2003, after the murder of policeman Stephen Oake,*
*who was fatally stabbed during an arrest*

God made him who had no sin to be sin for us, so that in him we might become the righteousness of God.

2 CORINTHIANS 5:21

How can you die, yet still talk? According to the Bible, it's possible. We read this about Abel: 'And by faith he still speaks, even though he is dead' (Hebrews 11:4).

The truth of this hit me with renewed force yesterday through three men who are now dead.

This week marked the anniversary of the birth of world champion athlete, Eric Liddell. His amazing story was told in the Oscar-winning film *Chariots of Fire*. He refused to run in the heats of the 100 metres in the Paris Olympics because they were held on a Sunday, yet he went on to become a world record holder at 400 metres. He spent the next 20 years in relative obscurity as a missionary in China. During World War II, he resisted all advice to move to safety, was captured by the Japanese and died in a prison camp in 1945, aged 43.

The second man, Ronald Sturt, died earlier this month. He played an important part in helping people stay in touch with the world through newspapers. Ron was the founder of *Talking Newspapers*, an innovative scheme that enables a quarter of a million blind or visually impaired people to enjoy the contents of their favourite paper or magazine.

Ron saw the idea in action on a visit to Sweden in 1970 and realized its potential to enrich people who are often marginalized. He began small in North Wales with the help of volunteers, and the idea spread. Ron fostered the vision and *Talking Newspapers* took off nationwide. Throughout his life, he maintained an active interest in a variety of groups serving people with disabilities.

Stephen Oake had no knowledge last weekend that his face and name would become national news within a few days. We all wish they hadn't. This brave police officer was killed in the line of duty and leaves a devastated circle of family and friends. In the many tributes to him, there is a consistent note about his qualities as a man, a husband, a father and a policeman.

Eric, Ronald and Stephen make an unlikely trio, but they are bound together by two ties—first, a strong Christian faith, and second, a desire to express that faith in a life of service for others.

Beyond death, their lives speak. Loudly.

## For further reading

PHILIPPIANS 3:1–12

However good and upright a life we live, it is not enough to put us right with God. As James 2:10 expresses it, 'Whoever keeps the whole law and yet stumbles at just one point is guilty of breaking all of it.' Only one man was entirely without sin, and that was Jesus. That is why, when we strap on the breastplate of righteousness, it is Christ's righteousness and not our own that we should be wearing (Philippians 3:9).

From the outside, some people look more righteous than others. Paul declared that if it was just about comparing ourselves with other people, then he could feel more confident than most (v. 4), but whoever we are, any breastplate comprising our own righteousness would be full of holes and leave us vulnerable. We can be confident only if we are equipped with the breastplate of Jesus' righteousness. This does not give us an excuse to give up trying to live a good life, however; we should continue to strive to please God and live the kind of life he intended for us (v. 12).

## Prayer

*Lord, I often sin and let you down but I am trusting in the righteousness of Jesus, which I have received by faith. Help me now to work out the implications of that by living well for your glory.*

# The readiness that comes from the gospel of peace

*Written in January 1998*

So, if you think you are standing firm, be careful that you don't fall!
1 CORINTHIANS 10:12

This weekend, world attention will focus on the island of Cuba. In a historic visit, Pope John Paul II and communist dictator Fidel Castro will embrace, and an estimated 3000 foreign journalists will report on a series of religious services.

Such events were unthinkable a few years ago. Forty years of militant communism has dominated every aspect of Cuban life, and the Christian church there has had its share of pressure. This is hardly surprising for a state that came to regard the words of Lenin as gospel, for he wrote, 'Everyone must be an atheist. We will never attain our goal until the myth of God has been removed from the thoughts of men.'

As Comrade Fidel and his friends have discovered, you can't erase the indelible. A fervent religious faith has flourished in Cuba, in spite of opposition. This week I listened to a BBC reporter relating stories of growth in various religious movements on the island, the largest being among evangelical Christians.

In Havana's Plaza de la Revolucion, the symbolic heart of Castro's regime, a new image has been added as part of the papal preparations. Alongside a statue to Jose Marti and a bronze sculpture of Che Guevara, two of Cuba's greatest heroes, another portrait has appeared. The figure of Jesus now dominates the square, bearing the slogan 'Jesus Christ, in you we trust.'

I am reminded of an event in the Chinese city of Chungking during the Cultural Revolution of the 1960s. Bibles, prayer and hymn books were confiscated and publicly burned. Christians were forced to watch this denunciation of their faith. Yet someone managed to conceal a charred page from a bonfire and it became a prized possession among the persecuted church. This single page from the Bible was read and reread among congregations for years. Its very preservation became, to the suffering church, a symbol of hope.

Years later, as China began to open its doors to the world, a Western Christian leader checked the story's authenticity. He was particularly keen to discover what part of the Bible had sustained the church throughout the lonely years of persecution.

The page was part of Matthew's Gospel which contains the following prophetic statement of Jesus: 'I will build my church, and the gates of hell will not overcome it' (Matthew 16:18). That's something to ponder as we witness some remarkable scenes in Cuba this weekend.

## For further reading

PHILIPPIANS 4:4–9

To play certain sports well, appropriate footwear is required. Similarly, the Roman soldier needed to wear footwear designed to enable him to stand his ground in battle. Most of us can't walk very far without our shoes.

So how can we obtain the peace that will enable us to persevere in our Christian walk? In this passage, Paul talks about three ways in which believers can receive God's peace: through prayer (v. 6), by meditating on what is good (v. 8) and by putting our faith into practice (v. 9). We have far more resources than the Chinese church with their one page from the Bible, and we do not face the same challenges to our faith as the church in Cuba has for decades. Even so, we should not be complacent. Paul advises us to be ready.

## Prayer

*Bring your anxieties to God and receive his peace, in the knowledge that when the time comes, he will enable you to stand firm.*

# The shield of faith

This is the victory that has overcome the world, even our faith.

1 John 5:4

There is a much-quoted Bible verse that says, 'They will beat their swords into ploughshares and their spears into pruning hooks' (Isaiah 2:4). This week I read a modern application of this ancient promise— not so much swords into ploughshares, more missile silos into churches. Let me explain.

During the final years of the former Soviet Union, a group of Christians from the city of Kobryn requested permission to construct a church building. When communism was at the height of its power, this would have been impossible, but times were changing.

The Byelorussian authorities granted permission and, due to the desperate shortage of building materials, made an unusual gesture. The group were invited to demolish a disused barracks and missile silo and to salvage any bricks, blocks and steel for use in their new building.

As they set to work on the demolition, an empty artillery shell was discovered, sealed into a brick wall. It had been tucked away as a time capsule when the barracks and silo had been built some 42 years earlier.

Among other papers in the capsule, a letter was discovered, part of which said, 'These bricks come from Polish Orthodox and Russian Orthodox churches. If this complex is ever torn down, we ask that the bricks be used to build churches.'

The churches referred to in the letter were demolished under Joseph Stalin's reign of terror. In such a climate of religious intolerance and persecution, the anonymous writers' secret request would have been laughable and naïve in the extreme. But, as the poet Henry Wadsworth Longfellow expressed it:

*Though the mills of God grind slowly, yet they grind exceeding small;*
*Though with patience He stands waiting, with exactness grinds He all.*

This true story is a reminder that faith is not so much a destination as a journey. There are often circumstances that seem stacked against the possibility that our dreams will ever be fulfilled. Prayer seems little more than wishful thinking and there are days when our doubts seem bigger than our beliefs.

On days like that, we do well to remember one of God's names: the Almighty.

In Geneva, there stands a monument to the Protestant Reformation that bears a telling inscription: 'One man with God is always in the majority.'

## For further reading

1 PETER 1:13–21

What are you putting your faith in? Your own sufficiency and ability to meet crises, other people, a programme your church has devised, or even in faith itself? Peter tells us that our 'faith and hope are in God' (v. 21). Only faith in Almighty God will protect us from the 'flaming arrows' with which 'the evil one' will try to demoralize and destroy us (Ephesians 6:16).

We do not know when we will be attacked or in what way, so we need to be 'self-controlled and alert' at all times. Since 'the devil prowls around like a roaring lion looking for someone to devour' (1 Peter 5:8), we should not be surprised or discouraged by his attacks. Rather than dreading these times, we should be ready with the shield of faith in our all-powerful God, who can bring about what seems impossible at the time and give us hope when all hope seems lost.

## Prayer

*Let all who take refuge in you be glad;*
*let them ever sing for joy.*

*Spread your protection over them,*
*that those who love your name may rejoice in you.*
*For surely, O Lord, you bless the righteous;*
*you surround them with your favour as with a shield.*

PSALM 5:11–12

# The helmet of salvation

But since we belong to the day, let us be self-controlled, putting on faith and love as a breastplate, and the hope of salvation as a helmet.

1 THESSALONIANS 5:8

I read an interview recently with the newly retired world champion triple jumper Jonathan Edwards, one of Britain's favourite sporting stars. But part of the interview jarred me badly. Let me quote: 'He is, and always has been, admirably courageous about breaking what is probably the last conversational taboo, worse than cursing, or belching—the mortifying fact of bringing up Jesus.'

I find it fascinating that in our proud, grown-up world of squeaky clean correctness, someone who (even from a non-believer's perspective) has made a lasting impression on history, shaped cultures and inspired great music, architecture, art and literature is now described as 'the last conversational taboo'.

Welcome to our brave new world where, in the hypermarket of spirituality and belief, anything to do with the 'J' word is kept under the counter and discreetly served in a plain brown wrapper. Believe anything you like, the weirder the better, but don't mention Jesus.

A hot topic for debate among church leaders currently is about new forms of church, and conferences, papers and discussions abound. A while ago, I reviewed another book that contributed to the conversation, and the title said it all: *Post-Christendom*. It posed the question, how can the Christian community in Europe adapt to a society that is interested in spirituality but not, so it seems, the organized church?

Whatever prescriptions are offered, most seem to agree that the personality and message of Jesus Christ must be at the centre.

Karl Barth, the famous Swiss-German theologian, was nearing the end of his life when he was invited to lecture at the University of Chicago Divinity School. At the conclusion, questions were invited and someone asked, 'Dr Barth, of all the things you have read, which has shown the most profound theological insight?'

Barth paused for a moment before quoting the words of a children's hymn: 'Jesus loves me, this I know, for the Bible tells me so.' This man of giant intellect, who had read hundreds of books and written tens of thousands of words, chose a kids' song that told a timeless truth.

Sorry if it breaches any new taboos, but without Jesus, the church has absolutely nothing worth offering that you can't find cheaper elsewhere and in a lot more comfortable surroundings. Jesus *is* the message.

## For further reading

PSALM 73

When the psalmist looked around him and saw 'the prosperity of the wicked', he was greatly discouraged, because they seemed to be better off than he was (vv. 12–14). But he was looking at the small picture, not the big one. When his 'heart was grieved' and his 'spirit embittered', he 'was senseless and ignorant'; when he looked to God, he saw clearly again (vv. 21–28). This is why the helmet of salvation is such an essential piece of armour in the Christian life. We need to protect our minds, our thoughts and our understanding from the attack of the evil one, who would try to convince us that the battle is too hard and not worth fighting.

In Romans 13:11, Paul encourages us by reminding us that 'our salvation is nearer now than when we first believed'. He is not saying that we do not have salvation right now; we received that when we came to faith in Christ (Ephesians 2:5). But it is also an ongoing process as we seek to grow in our Christian life (Philippians 2:12–13), and it is something that we will receive in full in the future when Jesus returns (1 Peter 1:5).

## Prayer

*Father, I pray for Christians who are tempted to give up on their faith because it seems too hard. Renew their hope in your salvation and remind them that they do not struggle alone, because you are with them and the final victory has already been won.*

# The sword of the Spirit

I have hidden your word in my heart that I might not sin against you.
PSALM 119:11

One of my first jobs on returning home from holiday is to read my mail. My efficient secretary usually groups letters into piles such as 'urgent', 'read only', 'for information' and so on. I'm thinking of suggesting two new categories: 'nice ones' and 'wear a crash helmet before reading'.

As most of us know, not all letters are pleasant to read. Still, I was heartened to learn this week that the Prime Minister apparently receives 500,000 letters a year at 10 Downing Street, and I'm sure they're not all wishing him a happy holiday.

I visited a friend yesterday who has undergone extensive hospital treatment and has now been discharged. I found her propped on the settee, surrounded by a pile of letters and cards. She was rereading them one by one and putting them into scrapbooks as a permanent reminder of the love and friendship that have helped her through a difficult patch.

All of this reminds me of the power and potential of words. 'The pen is mightier than the sword' is not a trite statement when viewed through the lens of history. Adolf Hitler's political testament, *Mein Kampf*, is not a very long book, but for every word in it thousands died in the bloody conflagration of World War II, proving that words do have consequences.

Most of the New Testament is taken up with a collection of letters, 21 of them in all. Part of their fascination is found in discovering the exact circumstances that caused them to be written. Most were addressed to churches and some to specific leaders. Often they deal with particular problems or questions, with the central aim of helping people to grow in their Christian faith.

One letter seems an odd fit among the rest: it's a piece of personal correspondence that doesn't appear to deal with any big church crisis. The Christian leader Paul wrote to a man called Philemon, asking for mercy on behalf of a runaway slave. In effect, it is a plea for the slave's life and serves as a reminder that true faith should touch our relationships.

The power of the written word is immense. It can heal or hurt, curse or bless, demean or encourage. Jesus said that what comes out of our mouths reveals what's in our hearts. And I guess the same is true of our pens.

## For further reading

MATTHEW 12:34; 2 TIMOTHY 2:14–19

The Roman sword that Paul would have had in mind when he spoke of 'the sword of the Spirit, which is the word of God' (Ephesians 6:17) was the lethal weapon with which the Roman soldier went into the heart of battle. God's word is not to be taken lightly, because it is 'living and active. Sharper than any double-edged sword, it penetrates even to dividing soul and spirit, joints and marrow; it judges the thoughts and attitudes of the heart' (Hebrews 4:12). It can be quite simply life-changing, and we should treat it with care and respect.

Paul instructed Timothy to do his best to be someone who 'correctly handles the word of truth' (2 Timothy 2:15). We should come to God's word seeking to hear what he wants to say to us through it, even if it is not necessarily what we would like to hear. And if we are to wield the sword of the Spirit, we should come often.

## Prayer

*I have chosen the way of truth;*
*I have set my heart on your laws.*
*I hold fast to your statutes, O Lord;*
*do not let me be put to shame.*
*I run in the path of your commands,*
*for you have set my heart free.*

PSALM 119:30–32

# Keep on praying

And pray in the Spirit on all occasions with all kinds of
prayers and requests.

EPHESIANS 6:18

The great car manufacturer, Henry Ford, was playing golf one day with three close friends. During the game, Ford mentioned that he had just taken out a substantial life insurance policy on himself. One of his playing partners was the boss of an insurance company and, feeling a little offended, protested, 'Henry, we're close friends and you know I'm in the business. Why did you go to someone else?' Ford answered, 'Because you never asked me!'

It's strange that we may be silent to the very people who need to hear what we have to say. My day, like most people's is, full of words and noise, much of it generated by myself, but I often miss saying the really important stuff.

For example, there's a straightforward 'thank you', which is a simple comment of appreciation that costs nothing, yet can mean so much. Then there's 'Can I help?' That can be a lifeline to someone struggling to manage alone. But one of my favourite phrases is 'Count on me', which is all the more special when it comes from someone you know really means it.

I was in conversation with a friend recently who said that no one ever told him how he was doing at his job. The sound of silence, for him at least, had been interpreted as disapproval. I told him my theory that if people aren't complaining, you should take it that they're happy. They'll soon let you know if you're wrong!

Henry Ford and his friend do more than remind us about the value of communication with each other. Their story is an echo of a verse in the Bible that stresses the importance of communicating with God. It is a blunt statement: 'You do not have, because you do not ask God. When you ask, you do not receive, because you ask with wrong motives, that you may spend what you get on your pleasures' (James 4:2–3).

Of course, there is the old chestnut that gets hauled out at such times: 'If God is all-knowing, then why bother to pray? He knows what we need anyway.' But such an argument shows a misunderstanding of the deeper meaning. Prayer at its very best is the language of relationship.

So don't just sit there. Ask.

## For further reading

EPHESIANS 6:18–20; 2 CORINTHIANS 1:3–11

Once we have 'put on the full armour of God', Paul gives us one further, crucial instruction: 'And pray...' (Ephesians 6:18). We may find prayer difficult to get down to, and difficult to do, but we are not left to struggle on our own. We have God's Holy Spirit to help and guide us. We must not forget that a soldier does not go out to battle alone, and we should pray for those on the battlefield with us. Our own struggles with the enemy should not blind us to the difficulties of others or make us selfish in our prayers. And, however great or important we may become, we are never beyond the need of prayer for ourselves, although it sometimes takes humility to ask for it, especially if it means admitting to a weakness that we would rather keep hidden.

In verses 19 and 20, Paul asks for specific prayer for himself. This is not just a polite request to make the Ephesian Christians feel involved in his ministry; Paul is convinced that God's help and deliverance come because of the prayers of his people (2 Corinthians 1:10–11). What greater encouragement do we need to 'be alert and always keep on praying for all the saints'?

## Prayer

*Pray for Christians who are in prison for their faith, as Paul was: that they might know God's presence with them at all times, that they might not be anxious, and that they might continue to declare their faith fearlessly.*

# Prayer and Praise

# Teach us to pray

'Your Father knows what you need before you ask him.'
MATTHEW 6:8

Mark Twain was famous for his humour. One night, while he was abroad on his travels, a group of friends decided to send him a birthday greeting. None of them knew his exact location, so they addressed the letter to 'Mark Twain, God knows where.'

Several weeks later, they received an acknowledgment from the great man that simply read: 'He did!'

We may be stunned at the wonders of a postal system that could track someone down so precisely but, personally speaking, I'd not be very chuffed if I'd slipped off to get away from it all, only to discover that I hadn't got away from anything.

Mark Twain's witty response not only reveals a sharp sense of fun but also a pretty good grasp of theology. God knew where he was, long before the postal service found him.

King David wrote many of the psalms, and one of the most often-quoted of them deals with the remarkable idea that every detail of our lives is known to God. 'O Lord, you have searched me and you know me. You know when I sit and when I rise; you perceive my thoughts from afar. You discern my going out and my lying down; you are familiar with all my ways. Before a word is on my tongue you know it completely, O Lord' (Psalm 139:1–4).

The truth is that God knows us better than we know ourselves, and several things follow from that. First, we don't have to explain how we are or what we feel—he knows. Second, it is useless to pretend or cover up—he knows. And third, the flimsy fabric of excuse can't hide the facts—he knows.

There is a fourth truth locked away in this astounding claim that God knows and understands us. It is expressed in the story of a little boy helping his dad on a flying visit to the supermarket at closing time. Ignoring the trolleys and baskets, dad grabbed what was needed and handed it to his son, who was obviously used to this last-minute dash. A passing shopper, who could see that the boy was struggling with an armful of goods, offered her trolley.

She was met with a shy smile and an incisive comment: 'No thanks. I'm OK. My dad knows how much I can carry.'

You see, he really does know.

## For further reading

MATTHEW 6:5–14

Jesus' followers must have seen a stark contrast between the religious élite of the day, with their showy, public prayers, and Jesus' habit of slipping off to lonely places to be alone with his Father. Our praying should be done in private, not looking over our shoulder to make sure everyone else is aware of how pious we are. And there is no need for long, eloquent prayers to persuade God to grant our requests, because he already knows what we need.

Having told us how not to pray, Jesus goes on to illustrate how we ought to pray. First, we need consciously to acknowledge our awareness of God's presence and of who he is (v. 9), and express our desire for his will to be worked out in our lives (v. 10). We are not to be greedy and grasping but should simply ask for what we need right now (v. 11). We should not come before God in prayer if we are holding grudges against other people. We need to forgive them first and then confess our own unworthiness and need of forgiveness (v. 12). Finally, we need to ask for God's protection, because we are weak and vulnerable (v. 13).

Prayer is not just words; prayer is about how we live.

## Prayer

*Our Father in heaven,*
*hallowed be your name.*
*Your kingdom come,*
*your will be done*
*on earth as it is in heaven.*
*Give us today our daily bread.*
*Forgive us our debts,*
*as we also have forgiven our debtors.*
*And lead us not into temptation,*
*but deliver us from the evil one.*

# Praise perspective

Let everything that has breath praise the Lord.
PSALM 150:6

What annoys you? According to a poll published last week, we Brits have a long list of irritations. Top of the poll came junk mail (65 per cent of those questioned included this), followed by motorists who hog the middle lane of motorways (34 per cent), companies where the phone is answered by recorded messages (33 per cent) and people who use mobile phones in public places (29 per cent).

I was so intrigued that I conducted my own research with a few friends, and discovered a fascinating list of pet hates. They included people who don't close doors, children who leave clothes lying around, and friends who telephone in the middle of a meal with the question 'Are you eating?' and then talk on as your dinner goes cold.

So what is guaranteed to raise your temperature to boiling point? And, more important, why?

I find that most of my personal irritations arise from a lack of perspective. I get cross about things that are not really important. The fact that Plymouth has an epidemic of red traffic lights is not the greatest injustice in the world. Murphy's well-known law, that the supermarket queue you choose always moves slower than the one next to it, won't shorten my life unless I let it.

When I come across people facing real problems in their lives, I find that my minor difficulties vanish like a mist. Just yesterday, I spoke to a friend about to leave England for a visit to a country in the developing world. His work will take him to some of the poorest slums on earth. He was bracing himself for a few weeks of emotional turmoil and asked if I had any advice to offer. 'Be prepared to see life through different eyes,'

I said, 'and be grateful for the chance to get things into proper perspective.'

Much of my moaning comes from a root of selfishness that distorts an accurate view of life. Left unchecked, it can sour and spoil everything. There's a Victor Meldrew in all of us that needs to be tamed. In the words of an old prayer, I find myself asking God, 'Give us, we pray, such a sense of all your mercies that our hearts may be unfeignedly thankful.'

'Unfeignedly' means without pretending. Honest thankfulness, you see, is a wonderful cure for moaning minnies.

## For further reading

PSALM 148:1–14

There is nothing like praise to change our perspective and to take our minds off ourselves. In this psalm, the whole of God's creation is shown to be praising him, from the 'heights above' (v. 1) to the 'ocean depths' (v. 7). There is something so extravagant about the praise described here that we can only be filled with wonder and awe as we realize that praise to God never ceases. From the 'heavenly hosts' (v. 2) down to 'small creatures and flying birds' (v. 10), all creation praises him—even the weather (v. 8). And all humankind is called to praise, from the most powerful (v. 11) to the smallest child (v. 12).

At this point, the psalmist reminds us that, as magnificent as creation is, God's splendour is even greater and 'his name alone is exalted' (v. 13). Then, in the final verse, we are told that God 'has raised up for his people a horn, the praise of all his saints' (v. 14), hinting at the coming of Jesus. Let us all, as 'people close to his heart', praise him.

## Prayer

*Praise the Lord.*
*Praise God in his sanctuary;*
*praise him in his mighty heavens.*
*Praise him for his acts of power;*
*praise him for his surpassing greatness.*

PSALM 150:1–2

# Does prayer work?

Then Jesus told his disciples a parable to show them that they
should always pray and not give up.

LUKE 18:1

'Does prayer work?' is a question I am often asked. My answer is yes,
but not always in the way we expect.

As many of us have discovered first-hand, there is no such thing as
a slot machine prayer—drop in the request, pull the handle and wait
for the answer to fall.

Søren Kierkegaard, the Danish philosopher, told a story of a boy
studying maths, whose teacher gave him a book of test questions. He
was told to work through the test but, on his honour, not to look at the
back of the book where the answers were given. He was told to work
out the problems himself.

The boy set about the task but temptation got the better of him and
he looked at the back of the book for the answers. He handed in his
exercises with a stunning array of correct answers. Kierkegaard pointed
out that the lad may have achieved good grades but he never succeeded
in learning mathematics. The moral is clear: as difficult as it may prove
to be, the way to succeed is to work out the answers for yourself.

I have two close friends who have taken a big decision this week. They
have been praying for months about the right choice to make. In their
own words, they have been looking for 'a flash of revelation', but have
been disappointed because no such thing has happened. They have made
their decision now, though, and I happen to think it is the right one. I also
think that they have had their revelation, but without the flash.

There are times when we pray and, almost like the boy in the story,
we want to look up the answer quickly in the back of the book.

Of course, there are occasions when prayers are answered suddenly, dramatically, miraculously. But a lot of the time, it is about working through to the solution, the long, slow, hard way. That means a few crossings out and much chewing of the end of the pencil.

Prayer in that setting takes on a whole new dimension. It's more about patience, trust and dogged persistence than quick answers. It's how the best mathematicians work—and it's also how the best saints are made.

## For further reading

MATTHEW 15:21–28

Jesus had ignored the Canaanite woman for so long that her persistence had begun to annoy the disciples. They asked him to get rid of her. When he finally spoke, it was to rebuff her, but still she didn't give up. She simply came closer and knelt before him, asking for help. His response seemed only to emphasize a disinclination to do what she asked, but even this did not put her off, and in that moment Jesus acknowledged her faith and granted her request.

Sometimes prayer feels as though we are battering on the door of heaven and nothing is getting through. It's so hard not to give up, but we have nowhere else to go and no other hope. When we persist in asking, we are being obedient (Luke 18:1) and demonstrating our faith.

## Prayer

*If you have been praying for a long time and seem no closer to an answer, pray whichever one of the two prayers below best fits your situation now.*

*Thank you, almighty Father, for renewing my faith to go on praying with so little visible encouragement and no answer yet. I believe you will answer my prayer.*

*Lord, give me renewed faith to go on praying. I feel like giving up but I have nowhere else to go.*

# Inspiration

*Written in July 2000*

When I tried to understand all this, it was oppressive to me
till I entered the sanctuary of God.

PSALM 73:16–17

Success, it is claimed, is due to one per cent inspiration and 99 per cent perspiration.

The World Cup these past few weeks seems to bear that out, as teams have sweated through matches in hot and humid conditions. The England team's achievements have been considerable but when you consider the weather conditions in which they normally play, their performance has been outstanding. Theirs is indeed achievement through perspiration!

Then there is the army of teenagers who are nearing the end of the annual exam marathon. Many of them are discovering that exams are often like life: you get out what you put in.

But I have been thinking this week about the other side of the equation—not so much the perspiration but the inspiration. Putting it simply, where do you find it when you need it?

My thinking was sparked by a psychologist's observation that when we have wrestled with a problem for a long time, yet failed to arrive at a solution, the answer often comes when we stop thinking about the issue and just relax. He recalled a conversation with one of the world's leading physicists, who told him, 'We often talk about the three Bs—the bus, the bath and bed. That's where great discoveries are made in our science.'

The mind is a fascinating instrument, but to get the best out of it we need to learn the skill of loosening as well as tightening its strings.

There is a prayer in the Bible that graphically describes an inspiration moment. It was written by someone struggling with the age-old problem: why do good things happen to bad people and bad things happen to good people? The sheer unfairness of it all had soured his heart and his relationships, with the result that he ended up feeling bitter and twisted.

Then came the inspiration moment. He describes it this way: 'When I tried to understand all this, it was oppressive to me till I entered the sanctuary of God.'

I have been around the block too many times to claim that God will always answer every question. Such a claim is both untrue and unhelpful. But if it is inspiration you seek, then the presence of the living God is the surest place to find it.

## For further reading

1 KINGS 3:10–28

Although Solomon was the king of a nation so great that the people were 'too numerous to count' (v. 8), and although he was related to Pharaoh king of Egypt (v. 1) and sought after by other important royal figures (5:1; 10:1), in this early part of his reign we see him dealing with two women who must have been among the lowliest of his subjects. How surprising that two prostitutes (NIV) should have had access to the king, let alone that he should have taken the trouble to give this inspired solution to their problem. It reminds us that God, the all-powerful king of heaven, also has time for us, whoever we are, when we come to him with our questions and problems. He is not the God of the great and powerful alone. The smallest child is important to him (Matthew 18:4). What matters is that we come without preconceived ideas of how he should answer but with openness to what he wants to say, because, like Solomon, he might well surprise us.

## Prayer

*Great God of heaven, who am I that you should hear my prayers? Thank you that Jesus' death has opened the way for me to come freely and without fear into your presence.*

# Transformations

# Good out of evil

Because of the Lord's great love we are not consumed, for his compassions never fail.

LAMENTATIONS 3:22

It is a shock when someone expresses publicly what you have been thinking privately. It happened to me one evening as I watched a TV news report of President Bush visiting a factory in Maryland and delivering an upbeat speech. He made personal reference to his own religious faith, which teaches him 'that good can come out of evil'.

The same thought had been running through my head most of that day, so hearing it articulated by the US President offered the scary thought that my house may be bugged by the CIA.

Truth to tell, George Bush and I are not alone in this view. It stands among several arguments that are offered in the complex philosophical discussion on the nature of evil and the problem of suffering.

Ask anyone who has faced a tough time, and often they will point to acts of kindness and love they have received, which brought strength and comfort. Those who survived the Blitz or stood shoulder to shoulder with others in the heat of battle talk of friendship and community spirit forged in a way unknown in more peaceful times.

An African proverb says, 'Smooth seas do not make skilful sailors' and although few would put up their hands and volunteer for adversity, we know that it produces some special skills in us and in others around us as well.

There is a letter in the New Testament nicknamed 'the epistle of joy'. In four brief chapters, the words 'joy' or 'rejoice' occur 13 times. Joy is the underlying theme of a letter written to a group of Christians struggling to work out their faith in a hostile world.

The author was the church leader Paul, who at the time of writing was in prison in Rome, under heavy military guard and facing the real prospect of execution. Everything around him and his readers spelt uncertainty. They had every reason to feel deeply insecure.

Paul doesn't set out to write his letter with joy as the theme; he has other things in view. But on every page it spills out. One telling phrase identifies the fuel on which he's running in this time of real crisis: 'I can do everything through him who gives me strength' (Philippians 4:13).

True faith is not escapism. It is about the capacity to stand and work to the end, so that even from evil, good things can come.

## For further reading

LAMENTATIONS 3:1–24

The Bible doesn't give a definitive explanation or reason for suffering. If we read it thoughtfully, we find that it addresses the problem in different ways, but why God allows suffering still remains essentially a mystery. Although Jeremiah was faithful to God, he still suffered exile with the rebellious Israelites. In this passage in Lamentations, he ascribes his suffering to God, and for the first 20 verses of the chapter we are made vividly aware of how painful it is. Then, from verse 21 onward, he turns his focus from himself to God. It is as though he is saying, 'This is how my suffering looks to me right now, but I'm going to suspend judgment for a while because I know that God is loving, unfailingly compassionate and faithful' (vv. 22–24). He chooses to 'wait quietly for the salvation of the Lord' (v. 26).

Many years later, Jesus came and suffered in a way that he did not deserve, on behalf of people who have rebelled against God. Jesus is God's answer when we think he doesn't care. What more proof do we need that he loves us?

## Prayer

*Almighty God, because of your love we are not consumed. Your compassions never fail. They are new every morning; great is your faithfulness.*

# Masterpieces in the making

I always pray with joy... being confident of this, that he who began a good work in you will carry it on to completion until the day of Christ Jesus.

PHILIPPIANS 1:4, 6

What's the connection between a tea stain and a muddy West Country field? I need to explain the link with a story I read some years ago.

In a small fishing village, a group of men were enjoying a drink at an inn. As the barmaid squeezed by, carrying a tray of tea in her hands, one of the men swung around and sent everything flying. The teapot smashed, leaving an ugly brown stain on what had been a nicely painted wall.

As they cleaned up the damage, it was obvious that the stained wall would need repainting. Then a stranger in the bar made an odd offer. He asked if he could have some time to work on the stain, and the landlord agreed.

Picking up a box, the stranger went to the wall and set to work. From the box he produced a collection of jars, brushes, paints and pencils and, with a fascinated audience watching his every move, he set to work.

When he finished, everyone agreed that the results were stunning. The ugly mark had been transformed to become the centrepiece of a picture that portrayed a stag sporting a magnificent set of antlers. The stain, although still visible, had been blended into a wall painting that made it look planned rather than accidental.

The artist signed the picture, paid for his meal and left. Only after he had gone did they study the autograph: E.H. Landseer. Sir Edwin Landseer, the famous wildlife artist, had been the mystery guest who turned a disaster into a masterpiece.

So what about the connection with a muddy field?

You may remember reading about the two men playing with a metal detector in Glastonbury, who uncovered a treasure trove of Roman coins. They became the legal owners of, according to the experts' assessment, one of the best finds of its kind.

A friend called earlier today to share some bad news, and asked me to pray for him as he copes with a number of difficulties. In response, I am trying hard to focus on two things: first, that God would surprise him so that he finds some unexpected 'treasure' in his pressures, and second, that what seems to be an ugly stain will be turned into something beautiful.

Is this just sentimental optimism? Hope is a better word. After all, God specializes in masterpieces.

## For further reading

2 CORINTHIANS 3:4–18

Landseer saw a stag, not a stain, and when God looks at us with our ugly, sin-damaged lives, he sees people who were lovingly created in his image, who need redemption and transformation to live lives that reflect him 'with ever-increasing glory' (v. 18). He sees possibilities in us that we are often unable to see for ourselves until we surrender our lives and begin to follow him. This is not to say that God wants us all to look alike and live similar lives. Just as his creation is rich and varied, so are the lives to which he calls us. We do not know the future, the unexpected directions our lives may take, the hardships and trials along the way, or the blessings and joys, but we do know that God 'who began a good work in you will carry it on to completion until the day of Christ Jesus' (Philippians 1:6). We are masterpieces in the making.

## Prayer

*Let Thy love my heart inflame,*
*Keep Thy fear before my sight,*
*Be Thy praise my highest aim,*
*Be Thy smile my chief delight.*

RALPH WARDLAW (1779–1853)

# Field of dreams

For we are God's co-workers; you are God's field, God's building.
1 CORINTHIANS 3:9

If modern technology is all it's cracked up to be, the next few columns will be coming to you from India.

Home to over 900 million people, India has woven a spell of enchantment for centuries. Having visited, travelled and even lived there for a short time, I never fail to be amazed by something new every day. Mark Twain put it better than anyone when he wrote of India:

*The land of dreams and romance, of fabulous wealth and fabulous poverty, of splendour and rags, of palaces and hovels, of famine and pestilence, of genii and giants and Aladdin lamps, of tigers and elephants, the cobra and the jungle, the country of a hundred nations and a hundred tongues, of a thousand religions and two million gods.*

That description was written in 1897 and in one sense little has changed in more than 100 years. But in another, things are so different.

Let me tell you one story of change that summarizes much of the dynamic potential to be found in the world's largest democracy. In 1982, I stood with an Indian friend in a field outside the city of Bangalore and he told me of his dream. With his newly acquired PhD, he could have taken his pick of top academic posts in the West, but he chose to put something back into the land that gave him birth.

I stood in the remains of that field a few days ago, as I have done several times in the intervening years. The buildings that now cover it are a nerve centre of activity stretching to various parts of this vast country. The centre provides training and teaching, medical care and practical help, development of cottage industries, a waste recycling project and a theological college. It remains unashamedly part of the Christian church in India but offers help to all, regardless of religion or caste. It works with the poorest of the poor in the slums and seeks to influence educators and legislators at the highest level.

A saying of Jesus has come home with renewed force this week. Comparing the minute mustard seed with the kingdom of heaven, he said, 'Though it is the smallest of all your seeds, yet when it grows, it is the largest of garden plants and becomes a tree, so that the birds of the air come and perch in its branches' (Matthew 13:32).

Yesterday, standing in the field of dreams, I could suddenly see what Jesus meant.

## For further reading

MATTHEW 13:31–32; 1 CORINTHIANS 3:5–9

A small seed contains within it the promise of something much larger and more attractive, but it is only experience that tells us so. The seed on its own looks very insignificant, the sort of thing we might thoughtlessly discard, but once it is planted in the ground, unseen, God is at work. Slowly, in its own time, the plant begins to grow from the seed.

Each of us is an imperfect part of God's perfect plan, but he can take our obedience in small things and knit it together with what others are doing, in order to bring about much greater things of which we could only have dreamed. Much of God's work takes place out of sight. He moulds us to his purposes from within, using all the circumstances of our lives and experiences, even our failures, and it is only in eternity that we shall come to full flowering. In the meantime, he is pleased to use us and to work, sometimes despite us, to bring blessing to others and ourselves if we are only alert to his voice and obedient to his call.

## Prayer

*Lord, I am so glad that you see the promise in my imperfect life and are willing to use even me.*

# Hope out of despair

We look for justice, but find none; for deliverance, but it is far away.
ISAIAH 59:11

This week I received letters from two friends. The first is a journalist, who enclosed a piece that he's written conveying how our world can be viewed as a global village. His article argues that if the world was shrunk to a village of one hundred people, with ratios similar to the five billion-plus on the planet, the neighbourhood would look something like this: 57 Asians, 21 Europeans, 14 from the Western hemisphere (North and South) and eight Africans; 51 females, 49 males; 70 non-whites, 30 whites.

Fifty per cent of the village's entire wealth would be in the hands of six people. Eighty would live in substandard housing and 70 would be unable to read. Fifty would suffer from malnutrition. One would have a college education and no one would own a computer.

The second letter came from a friend recently returned from a harrowing visit to Rwanda. As head of a relief agency, he spearheads a team offering help to a population devastated by war. He estimates that 75 per cent of the country is made up of widows and orphans—victims of inter-tribal rivalry, which has sparked an orgy of murder.

He told of meeting Teresa, who was taken captive after her husband was murdered. Having been repeatedly raped, she was thrown into a deep pit, where she lay among dead bodies for three days, miraculously surviving the blast of a grenade thrown into the pit. My friend struggled to find words to express his emotions as he listened to women tell similar, appalling stories. He is a man well experienced in world poverty but concludes, 'I have never witnessed despair of the magnitude or nature that I encountered in Rwanda.'

The two letters sit side by side on my desk as I write. I feel overwhelmed and helpless in the face of such need. But I have decided on three courses of action. First, to pray with greater commitment for those in our world who suffer. Second, to redouble my efforts to promote and support those agencies that are fighting need in a credible way. And third, to resolve to do whatever is in my power to do, to turn our 'global village' into a place where all in the neighbourhood get a fairer share.

A knee-jerk reaction? Perhaps. But how else do we respond to God who declares, 'Defend the cause of the weak and fatherless; maintain the rights of the poor and oppressed' (Psalm 82:3)?

## For further reading

ISAIAH 61; LUKE 4:21

Jesus came as a light shining in the darkness of a sin-sick world. He came to bring us good news, to bind up our broken hearts, to free us from captivity to sin, to release us from the darkness of our unbelief, to replace mourning with gladness and despair with praise (Isaiah 61:1–3). How desperately our world needs this! When people made in God's image suffer unspeakable horror and torment, God does not watch from afar. He is right there. He is so grieved by the effects of sin that he did the unthinkable: he bore the punishment himself. We should never doubt his love. And we are called to be like him: to be grieved when sin causes others to suffer and to try to make a difference. We may think that there is very little we can do, but God can take even a little and multiply it for good.

## Prayer

*There was no other good enough*
*To pay the price of sin;*
*He only could unlock the gate*
*Of heaven and let us in.*

CECIL FRANCES ALEXANDER (1818–95)

# Clay pots

*Written in December 2002*

Yet, O Lord, you are our Father. We are the clay, you are the potter;
we are all the work of your hand.

ISAIAH 64:8

Benjamin Disraeli once offered the following definitions. 'The difference
between a misfortune and a calamity is this: if Gladstone fell into the
Thames, it would be a misfortune. But if someone dragged him out
again, that would be a calamity.'

According to some, the appointment of Rowan Williams as the new
Archbishop of Canterbury signals a future verging on the calamitous for
the Church of England. Personally, I'd rather give the man a chance. I
find it rather unreasonable that some people have been trying to get him
red-carded before he's even got his tracksuit off.

By all accounts, Williams is a man with a sharp mind and a deep faith.
I hope that is true, because both are essential requirements for a job that
offers more challenges than perks. But how does he feel as he takes office?

Listen to a remarkable statement that Rowan Williams made this
week: 'I know with absolute certainty that there are things at which I
shall fail... I won't do everything right... This is a challenge that I face
with a sense of inadequacy.' It is not often that someone embarking on
a top job does so with such a frank admission, which makes it all the
more essential that he is given every chance to prove himself.

There was a note of reality, too, in his admission that the Church's
obsession with status and hierarchy was 'profoundly anti-Christian'. We
can only hope that he proves to be a leader who gets to the station one
stop beyond rhetoric.

This week, I have been leafing through a new book. It is a biography of John Wesley, the founder of Methodism, written by the well-known politician, Roy Hattersley. The author and the subject make a strange combination: Hattersley is an agnostic, yet with a serious intent to probe behind an influential Christian character in British history.

The book is entitled *A Brand from the Burning* and it tells Wesley's story with skill and insight. One sentence stood out for me in this week when a new Archbishop takes office. It is a staggering assessment: 'Wesley was one of the architects of modern England... [his] second reformation created a new church and helped to build a new nation.'

New church, new nation? Yes, please.

## For further reading

1 KINGS 19:9–13; JEREMIAH 18:1–10

Do you feel inadequate? Are you trying hard to become a good enough Christian for God to use? God has an uphill task at times, getting our attention off ourselves so that we can pay attention to him. That's why it's often at our lowest times that we hear God most clearly—those times when we have given up trying to do things in our own strength because we have no strength left, when all our plans have come to nothing and we are utterly discouraged.

You may feel you have let God down, but the Potter hasn't finished with you yet. Jeremiah describes the potter taking the spoiled pot and, rather than putting it aside and starting with new clay, shaping it into another pot 'as seemed best to him' (v. 4).

If we are honest, a lot of our good works are attempts to justify ourselves to our heavenly Father. We know that our salvation is God's gift (Ephesians 2:8–9) but we still keep trying to earn it. Serving God is about learning to know him and following his direction, moment by moment, as we allow him to shape us as he thinks best.

## Prayer

*Father, thank you for your gentle hands, which shape me into the person you want me to be, transforming my flaws in your perfect design.*

# Setting today and tomorrow free

Be self-controlled and alert. Your enemy the devil prowls around like a roaring lion looking for someone to devour.

1 PETER 5:8

It's frightening how today and tomorrow can be imprisoned by yesterday. Two conversations and a pair of news stories illustrate that for me.

A friend shared sad news of a family row that has produced an icy silence and I offered my best wishes for a thaw. She shook her head and, referring to the main cause of the row, said, 'She doesn't do sorry, I'm afraid.'

Another friend asked a serious question about the power of words spoken in anger that can become like a curse on someone's life. Angry words, especially from someone in a place of respect, can wound deeply. 'You're useless. You'll never amount to anything. I'm ashamed of you' are words whose power lives on long after the person who said them has gone.

Now for the news stories. First, a remarkable report of a Chief Constable travelling all the way from Sussex to Liverpool to apologize to the family of a man who was wrongly shot dead in a raid several years ago. The family welcomed the move, which was seen as a proper acknowledgment that a grave injustice had been done.

The second story detailed a public ceremony held in Fiji this week, attended by relatives of the late Thomas Baker, who was a missionary killed and eaten by tribesmen in 1867. The event was attended by the Fijian Prime Minister and members of the influential council of great chiefs. Some travelled for five hours on foot to the site of the murder.

Leaders of the island community are convinced that the effects of the murder have blighted the village of Nubutautau ever since, and the service was a serious attempt to put matters right. Members of Baker's family were invited to the ceremony, where villagers wept openly as embraces of reconciliation were exchanged.

Fiji's Prime Minister, Laisenia Qarase, told the gathering, 'Your appreciation of the difficulties your people are facing and your tremendous effort is so critical in trying to solve them through turning to God and seeking his forgiveness for what was done to him and his servant the Rev Thomas Baker.'

Forgiveness and the power to move on are the 'get out of jail' cards that set today and tomorrow free. And there's just one hand that deals them.

## For further reading

ROMANS 8:1–4; 1 PETER 5:8–11

Many Christians are trapped in the past, unable to enjoy the freedom that God wants them to enjoy, because they look back to something they have done wrong and cannot forgive themselves. Even though God has offered the full and free forgiveness won by Christ on the cross, they feel that their sin is the exception. Even worse, perhaps they even committed the sin after becoming a Christian, making a blot on the clean heart they were given when they turned in repentance and faith to God.

We should not underestimate our enemy, the devil. He is intelligent and powerful and determined to ruin believers' lives. He goes straight for the points at which we are vulnerable, and the inability to forgive ourselves, together with the doubt that God could really forgive us, provide a perfect opportunity. But don't overestimate the devil's power either. 'Resist him, standing firm in the faith' (1 Peter 5:9), and remember that 'there is now no condemnation for those who are in Christ Jesus' (Romans 8:1).

## Prayer

*Reflect on the extent and horror of Jesus' sufferings on the cross and accept that they were adequate to pay the price for your sin. Forgive yourself because God has forgiven you.*

# Change is possible

Be imitators of God, therefore, as dearly loved children and live a life of love, just as Christ loved us and gave himself up for us as a fragrant offering and sacrifice to God.

EPHESIANS 5:1–2

Let me tell you a story of revenge.

Several years ago, a rabbi was shot in the head by a Palestinian terrorist in a Jerusalem street market. The man survived and his assailant was sent to jail. The terrorist's only regret was that he had failed to kill his 'chosen military target'.

The rabbi had been visiting Jerusalem, as his permanent home was in New York, and he returned there to recover from his injury. But his daughter vowed to get even with the man who had brought such suffering to her family.

She travelled to the Middle East and tracked down the terrorist's family. Claiming to be a journalist researching a story, she won their confidence and began to write to the jailed man who had attempted to kill her father.

Through correspondence, she asked some telling questions, such as, 'Can you describe the moment of the shooting and what you were feeling?' and 'What would you tell this man and his family if you met them today?' The questions came in the guise of dispassionate journalism, simply seeking background material for a story, and he had no idea that the journalist was the daughter of the man he had tried to murder.

Finally, the woman decided to reveal her true identity. She chose her time carefully. It was in the middle of a parole hearing for the terrorist, where she had gone to speak in *support* of his application for early release.

We can only imagine the stunned silence that greeted her revelation.

Laura Blumenfeld achieved a rare victory. Instead of inflicting more suffering, she forced her enemy to feel her own—and her strange actions reaped a remarkable reward. The terrorist, Omar Khatib, has now renounced violence. In a letter to Laura's father, he wrote, 'Laura was the mirror that made me see your face as a human person.'

Laura has written a book about her story, and it has a one-word title: *Revenge*. As one American reviewer commented, 'If only the Middle East had more vengeful people like her.'

Laura is Jewish and Omar a Muslim, but both exemplify something that is often forgotten in our complex world of religious prejudice, hatred and division: change is possible.

Thank God for Laura and people like her who, instead of cursing the darkness, choose to light a candle instead.

## For further reading

EPHESIANS 4:31—5:2, 8–16

When we forgive someone who has injured us, it is, in a way, like looking in a mirror and recognizing the potential for cruelty and selfishness that lives within each one of us. Through being forgiven, Omar Khatib was able to see his victim not as a faceless enemy but as a fellow human being. We all need forgiveness at some time, and if we are to enjoy the freedom for which 'Christ has set us free' (Galatians 5:1), we also need to forgive. Therefore we should rid ourselves of the 'bitterness, rage and anger, brawling and slander' and 'malice' that accompany an unforgiving attitude, and should become 'kind and compassionate' and 'forgiving'. In this way we will 'be imitators of God', reflecting his love to others (Ephesians 4:31—5:1).

Jesus told his followers to make forgiveness a priority (Matthew 5:24), just as he made it a priority for us (Ephesians 5:2). Forgiveness is liberating because it is about acknowledging the extent of our hurt and facing it, rather than denying it or trying to forget it. And when we have forgiven our enemy, it may then be possible—both for them and for us—to forget and move on.

## Prayer

*Lord Jesus, set me free from the hardness of heart that tells me some things are unforgivable. Although it may be difficult and take a long time, with your help I want to forgive those who have hurt me, just as you have forgiven me.*

# The Wicked Bible

*Written in October 2001*

The Lord detests those whose hearts are perverse but he delights
in those whose ways are blameless.

PROVERBS 11:20

Have you ever heard of 'The Wicked Bible'?

In 1631, a printer made an error that resulted in an unfortunate reading of one of the Ten Commandments. His omission of the word 'not' gave a whole new meaning to the seventh commandment, as his version stated, 'Thou shalt commit adultery.'

The printer was fined £300 (a huge sum in those days) and King Charles I issued an order for all copies to be destroyed, since when this particular translation has been dubbed 'The Wicked Bible'.

It makes you wonder what might have happened if the mistake had not been spotted.

This week, the Northern Ireland Secretary, John Reid, made a key-note speech at the Labour Party Conference. He reminded his listeners of the uncomfortable fact that terrorism continues to fester in our own backyard. He made this hard-hitting comment: 'Terrorism does not just appear in the desert carrying a Koran. It appears on the streets of Northern Ireland clasping a Bible.'

The Secretary of State is spot on, but if his diagnosis is correct I want to avoid any hasty prescriptions that might follow. It is not the use of the Koran or the Bible that is the problem, but the abuse of them.

Bigotry, racial prejudice and hatred of those who are different from ourselves are the dark side of human nature. The fact that those who are consumed by these things search for leaders, ideologies and religious writings to prop up their evil beliefs is nothing new.

Fanatical terrorists blow themselves up in suicide bomb attacks in the belief that they will be rewarded with the pleasures of paradise, but Islamic scholars tell us that this is a falsification of the Koran. Terrorists in Northern Ireland, on both sides of the sectarian divide, believe that their mission has divine approval. They too are wrong, and worse than wrong—blindly, arrogantly and religiously wrong.

In both cases, people have twisted words to suit themselves, or, like the printer of 'The Wicked Bible', changed the text to mean the opposite.

Jesus said that the whole of God's law could be summed up in two simple phrases: 'love God' and 'love your neighbour'.

A life lived by those two benchmarks is as far from wickedness as it is possible to get. And it's deeds, not creeds, that reveal the true fruit of faith.

## For further reading

ACTS 9:1–25

Just as good or simply neutral things can become harmful in the hands of wicked people, so even bad things and people can be transformed and used for good by our loving, holy God. Saul had developed from being an approving spectator at the martyrdom of Stephen (Acts 8:1) to a ruthless persecutor of those who followed Jesus, 'breathing out murderous threats against' them (9:1), but his encounter with Jesus left him helpless and blind, needing to be led by the hand like a small child.

At this stage we are introduced to Ananias, and in this brief scene we see the sort of man he was, one who, despite his natural doubts, took God at his word and obeyed him immediately, becoming the first Christian to meet the changed Saul (or Paul, as he was later invariably known). From then on, the zeal Paul had demonstrated in persecuting believers was transformed for God to use in his mission to take the gospel to those outside the Jewish faith.

Terrorism is an unspeakable evil, but we should not be surprised if God has a better plan to save and transform even the most hardened terrorist. We can pray for that.

## Prayer

*Lord, nothing is hidden from you. I pray that you would thwart the plans of the wicked and that you would reveal yourself and your love to them, that they might repent and follow you.*

# What can still be repaired

If it is possible, as far as it depends on you, live at peace with everyone.
ROMANS 12:18

The most solemn festival in the Jewish year is Yom Kippur, the Day of Atonement. Its roots go back into the Old Testament, when a national day of reflection, confession of sin and absolution was established.

We find the origin of the English word 'scapegoat' in the ancient ceremony. During the service, a goat was chosen and the high priest laid his hands on it and confessed the sins of the nation. The animal was then led away and released into the desert, offering a powerful picture of sin being confessed and carried away.

In recent years, Yom Kippur has been marked with violence in the Middle East. If ever there was a situation that cried out for a Day of Atonement, this is it—a time when anger, prejudice, hatred and the desire to avenge might be carried away and a new beginning established.

I've come across a prayer that is often used at Yom Kippur. It strikes me as a prayer that carries no religious label, that is accessible even to those unsure about what they believe. It's a prayer for a personal Day of Atonement.

*We have grown accustomed to sin and the fragments of Scripture lie shattered in our life; charity has withered with calculation and the sparks of purity have burnt out. Yet we still come on Yom Kippur and God who said, 'I have forgiven' whispers it again to us and waits for our reply.*

*What shall it be? What form will it take?*

*Let us repair what can still be repaired.*

*Let us give back the gain we earned by injustice.*

*Let us make peace with our injured brother.*
*Let us restore the person we wronged.*
*Let us admit what is false in ourselves.*
*Let us put right what is wrong in our family life.*
*Let us not sour the joy of living.*

*May God give us the courage to do these things and help us to rebuild our lives. And when we have finished our tasks, may He permit us to enjoy the light sown for the righteous so that He can delight in us.*

*The gates of his mercy are still open. Let us enter in.*


## For further reading

Luke 19:1–10

All Zacchaeus wanted was to catch a glimpse of Jesus as he passed through Jericho. Instead, he found himself with an uninvited but very welcome guest (vv. 5–6), and the event changed his life. One of the first things Zacchaeus wanted to do next was to 'give back the gain… earned by injustice'.

Most of us have regrets about times in the past when we have wronged others, whether intentionally or not, and although it takes courage to admit that we have been wrong and to try to put things right—especially if we think we won't get a very warm reception when we do—it is harder still to have to live with the knowledge that it is too late to do anything about it. Therefore, if you are able, 'repair what can still be repaired' while there is time; and if not, be consoled by remembering that 'the gates of his mercy are still open' and you may enter in.


## Prayer

*Come before God, who paid a high price to make peace with you through the death of Jesus on the cross, and thank him for the opportunity to repair any harm you have done to someone else. Then ask him for the courage and resolve to act on it.*

# Drink to remember

Do not get drunk on wine, which leads to debauchery.
Instead, be filled with the Spirit.

EPHESIANS 5:18

Three seemingly unconnected incidents drifted by me this week.

The first was a newspaper report of a man in Modesto, California, found lying in a pool of blood with a brick at his side. Police at first thought he was the victim of a mugging, but witnesses revealed a more bizarre explanation.

He was playing a game that involved throwing the brick high in the air and trying to avoid it when it made its return journey to earth. He was doing this at 2 am and, in the darkness, failed to spot the descending missile in time. The report ended with a classic 'police spokesman' line. 'We believe alcohol was involved' was the memorable quote.

Then there was my internet-potty friend who set off last weekend with his wife to a hotel that he had booked online. He had downloaded a general map of the area but they became hopelessly lost in the countryside. Pulling up at a village pub, his wife volunteered to seek directions. 'Give me the address,' she asked, and an embarrassed silence followed. In the rush to leave, he had scribbled down the name of the hotel and its postcode but no road address. I draw a veil over what happened next. Let's just say that it will take him some time to live it down.

My third chance encounter was with a man who admitted that he had made a total mess of his life and damaged a number of people along the way. I appreciated his honesty and encouraged him not to give up hope. But I was haunted by his admission that a relentless pursuit of happiness had only made him more miserable.

Jesus put his finger on the pulse of life when he said, 'Seek first [God's] kingdom and his righteousness, and all these things will be given to you as well' (Matthew 6:33).

Life is a gift that is offered on loan for a short time. We can waste it and spoil it or give it away and find it. The choice is ours. But to live blindly is like throwing a brick into the night sky.

Most of us want to live happy and fulfilled lives, but 'happiness' is too vague a postcode to get us there.

Jesus' words suggest a much more precise address.

## For further reading

ACTS 2:1–13

When Jesus was arrested, his disciples fled. As far as we know, only John was present at his crucifixion. After his death, they gathered together behind locked doors for fear of what might happen to them (John 20:19). What a difference the coming of the Holy Spirit made to them! Some people even accused them of being drunk (Acts 2:13). Instead of hiding away, they drew a curious crowd, and then Peter preached boldly to the gathered people.

Paul, in Ephesians, contrasts being drunk on wine with being filled with the Holy Spirit. Instead of the drunkenness that overcomes inhibitions and leads to debauchery (and unfortunate accidents with bricks), we are to be filled with the Spirit that leads to joy and boldness. Many people 'drink to forget', but whenever we celebrate the Lord's supper we drink to remember. Jesus' death brings healing for the past and hope for the future.

## Prayer

*Ask God to fill you anew with his Holy Spirit.*

# Faith and a good conscience

Though your sins are like scarlet, they shall be as white as snow; though they are red as crimson, they shall be like wool.

ISAIAH 1:18

Two pieces of information landed on my desk this week. The first was a report of a recent survey conducted with 11–18 year olds in the USA. It was a disturbing read, as the following selection of statistics shows.

Forty-five per cent of the youngsters agreed with the statement, 'Everything in life is negotiable.' Sixty-six per cent admitted to having lied to their parents in the past three months; 59 per cent said they had lied to their friends. Fifty-five per cent summarized their thoughts and feelings as 'confused' and 50 per cent admitted feeling 'stressed out' with life.

The second piece of information came in a book I had been asked to review, in which the author relates a true story.

In 1984, an Avianca Airlines jet crashed in Spain. Investigators studying the accident made an eerie discovery. The black box recorders revealed that several minutes before impact a shrill, computer-synthesized voice from the plane's automatic warning system had told the crew repeatedly in English, 'Pull up! Pull up!'

The pilot, evidently thinking the system was malfunctioning, snapped, 'Shut up, gringo!' and switched the system off. Minutes later, the plane ploughed into the side of a mountain. Everyone on board died.

I found myself asking the question: whatever happened to conscience? Like the Avianca pilot, we have become adept at switching off the disturbing voice that challenges our planned course of action, and we seem to learn that dangerous skill at an early age.

The consequences of a violated conscience lie all around us. Have you noticed, for instance, how we have more victims and fewer culprits these days?

The Puritan Richard Sibbes wrote in the 17th century that conscience is the soul reflecting on itself. Yet such a notion is dismissed as quaint and outmoded, belonging to an age of horses and highwaymen. In today's world, so we are told, guilt is definitely off the menu. The g-word is non-cool.

In stark contrast, the Bible teaches that the conscience is the early warning system that God gave us so that we could live with others—and ourselves—in harmony. We can train it and program it or ignore and violate it.

Paul, the famous Christian leader, warned a younger colleague of the importance of 'holding on to faith and a good conscience. Some have rejected these and so have shipwrecked their faith' (1 Timothy 1:19).

Faith and a good conscience—two indispensable gifts to carry with you on the flight deck.

## For further reading

PSALM 51:7–17

God cannot ignore our sin. We may try to do so, shutting our ears to the voice of conscience and pursuing our own course, heedless of where it might lead, seeking only to please ourselves in the present moment and postponing the inevitable feelings of guilt.

Perhaps there is present or past sin in your life that is 'like scarlet' to you, and you are totally overwhelmed with the shame, even if nobody else suspects it. You have let God and other people down and would give anything to turn back the clock and make different choices. You feel you have shipwrecked your faith, past hope of rescue. Listen to God's words in Isaiah: 'For a brief moment I abandoned you, but with deep compassion I will bring you back. In a surge of anger I hid my face from you for a moment, but with everlasting kindness I will have compassion on you' (Isaiah 54:7–8). God's mercy towards us never fails. Thank him.

## Prayer

*O God, do not despise my 'broken and contrite heart' (Psalm 51:17).*

# Family Matters

# Called to care

He was despised and rejected by others, a man of sorrows, and familiar with suffering.
ISAIAH 53:3

Peter Arnett was a reporter for CNN working in the West Bank when a bomb exploded. Panic broke out as people ran in every direction, some to offer help, others to escape the scene of carnage.

Arnett was confronted by a man holding a badly injured girl in his arms. The stranger pleaded, 'Please help us! I need to get her to hospital!' Arnett bundled them into his car and, waving his Press sticker, negotiated his way out of the area. The man cradled the injured girl, then exclaimed, 'Can you go faster? I'm losing her.'

They made it to the hospital in minutes and the reporter helped the man carry the girl inside. She was rushed into theatre and the two men waited anxiously in the corridor. It was not the time for conversation. They sat silently, hoping and praying.

After some time, a grim-faced doctor emerged. 'I am so sorry,' he told them. 'She has just died.' The man collapsed in tears and Arnett hugged him compassionately. Desperately searching for words, he mumbled, 'I don't know what to say. I can't imagine how you feel. I have never lost a child.'

The distraught man looked startled. 'Mister, that Palestinian girl was not my daughter. I'm an Israeli settler. That Palestinian is not my child. But there comes a time when each of us must realize that every child, regardless of their background, is a daughter or a son. There must come a time when we realize that we are all family.'

That true story reminds us of a couple of important things. First, don't judge a book by its cover. If we are not careful, we can end up making hasty judgments by thinking in headlines: 'All Muslims are terrorists; all teenagers are troublemakers; all single parents are spongers'. None of those statements is true.

Second, we can be so numbed by the acts of terror perpetrated by a few sick people that we miss the thousands of ordinary acts of kindness, silently repeated day after day across our world. Evil loves the limelight but doesn't deserve it.

Perhaps that Israeli settler reveals, in a simple sentence, a powerful weapon in the global fight against terrorism. It's called the human race—and we are all in it.

## For further reading

PSALM 22:1–21

Although King David wrote this psalm many years before the birth of Jesus, it is impossible to miss the foreshadowing of Jesus' crucifixion experience in it. Jesus himself cried out, 'My God, my God, why have you forsaken me?' (v. 1) in the agony of his death. Jesus, the 'man of sorrows... familiar with suffering', is able to identify with and understand the suffering that is in the world. As his followers, we are called to try to do the same.

You are probably reading this book somewhere fairly quiet, with no sense of imminent danger. Yet right now there are wars going on, violent acts being planned or committed, and people suffering from hunger, unjust imprisonment or sickness. We live in a media-saturated world and we cannot bury our heads in the sand. The maimed victim of a bombing, the bereaved mother in an earthquake, the husband keeping vigil over a dying wife, the child who has never known anything but war, the prisoner of conscience, these are all members of our family. God calls us to care.

## Prayer

*Watch, dear Lord, with those who wake, or watch, or weep tonight, and give your angels charge over those who sleep. Tend your sick ones, O Lord Christ. Rest your weary ones. Bless your dying ones. Soothe your suffering ones. Pity your afflicted ones. Shield your joyous ones. And all, for your love's sake.*
ST AUGUSTINE OF HIPPO

# A rainbow world

Do not oppress an alien; you yourselves know how it feels to be aliens, because you were aliens in Egypt.

EXODUS 23:9

Julie was the only female present at a high-powered meeting when the tea trolley arrived. The chairman, anxious not to interrupt the discussion, asked her, 'Would you mind playing mother for us?' as he nodded towards the trolley.

Julie stood and replied, 'Not at all', then changed her tone to soft and soothing and asked, 'Now, Tony, did you remember to put your vest on this morning, sweetheart?'

I am sure the red-faced Tony got the point. We all realize that political correctness has some loony aspects, but many of the changes in everyday behaviour and language have gone a long way towards breaking stereotypes about men and women. There is a growing awareness, too, about attitudes and words that can mask an insidious racism, but on this front there is still a long journey ahead.

Just a few days ago, a close friend witnessed a confrontation in a Plymouth store between two women. Out of the blue, a white woman told a brown woman that people like her were not welcome there. Blue, white and brown—I deliberately chose the words because colour was at the heart of the issue.

My friend, who is a mild-mannered woman, flipped her lid (her words, not mine) and told her fellow citizen what she thought of her behaviour. She then tracked down the embarrassed Asian shopper and apologized profusely that she had been so insulted.

A recent TV programme exposed the racism of a handful of police officers. To their great credit, the authorities concerned took swift and decisive action. So did my friend in the middle of a busy Saturday when she needn't have bothered.

A cluster of the laws given by God to Moses relate to the foreigners who found themselves living among the people of Israel. They were not to be oppressed or abused, and their rights were to be respected. The law said, 'Do not oppress an alien; you yourselves know how it feels to be aliens, because you were aliens in Egypt.'

Yes, we need rules about immigration, and proper controls are important, but a rainbow world needs people with a rainbow outlook. Sexism is wrong, and so is racism, plus a few other 'isms' as well.

And, by the way, Jesus was an Asian.

## For further reading

EXODUS 23:1–9

Standing up for what is right and just may mean being the only one to speak up. It takes courage. Being angry can help, although caution is needed in how we express our anger (Ephesians 4:26). This passage in Exodus talks about not following the crowd or being biased in favour of one person or another (vv. 1–3). It warns us not to be sucked into a certain type of behaviour in order to please other people or to pay someone back (v. 5).

The Israelites were urged to remember how it felt to have no rights and to be at the mercy of the Egyptians (v. 9). We too can recall social situations or times in our lives when we have felt like outsiders or been rejected, and these memories help us to empathize with others who find themselves suffering in this way now. A kind word, a smile, a considerate action—something small and not very costly—could really help someone who feels lonely and out of their depth. Thank God when he gives you the opportunity to make any small difference.

## Prayer

*I pray, Lord, for those who have come to this country to escape from unbearable situations in the place they used to call home. May they meet with kindness and understanding. May they know freedom from fear.*

*May bad memories fade and emotional and physical scars heal. And if I can help them in any way, Lord, show me how.*

# God with us

No one has ever seen God, but God the One and Only, who is at
the Father's side, has made him known.

JOHN 1:18

India is a land that runs rich with cultures and traditions.

In one Indian tribe, it was customary for a boy who reached the age
of 13 years to mark his transition to manhood by spending a night
alone in the jungle. One boy later recalled his gruelling ordeal. He had
been led into the depths of the jungle and left weaponless and alone.
He knew he had to 'prove' himself to his community by sitting quietly
until the sun rose. He didn't sleep a wink; every rustle of a tree or
unfamiliar sound forced images on his mind of some impending terror.
It was a night he would never forget.

As dawn began to break, strange shapes gradually became more
familiar. Then he noticed a very familiar shape. Seated behind a tree,
not more than 50 paces from where he had spent a terrifying night, sat
his father, with a loaded rifle.

He thought he had faced the test alone, but in fact his father had
spent the whole night watching over his boy. As the young man said
later, 'If I'd known my dad was there and that close, I wouldn't have
been frightened at all!'

One of the most beautiful psalms in the Bible uses a similar picture:
'I lift my eyes to the hills—where does my help come from? My help
comes from the Lord, the Maker of heaven and earth. He will not let your
foot slip—he who watches over you will not slumber; indeed he who
watches over Israel will neither slumber nor sleep' (Psalm 121:1–4).

This image of God as a watchful father occurs in other parts of the
Bible. Perhaps the most puzzling, yet most memorable, is the father in

the parable of the prodigal son. The son had left the family and blown his inheritance, but was now on the homeward trip, a broken man. We read, 'But while he was still a long way off, his father saw him' (Luke 15:20).

According to Jesus, even the rebellious son has a watchful father.

Suffering is a hard path and not an easy one to tread. One of the toughest parts of it is the feeling of aloneness. Although others can sympathize, pray and offer love, they can't walk inside our shoes.

But there is a Father who never sleeps and who takes the terror from the darkness.

## For further reading

ROMANS 11:33–36; JOHN 17:20–26

How can people like us know Almighty God, the Creator of heaven and earth? He is far above us. His judgments are 'unsearchable' (Romans 11:33). How can we know the mind of the one whose thoughts are not our thoughts, nor his ways our ways (Isaiah 55:8)? Is it really possible that the all-powerful, transcendent God would even want to be known by sinful men and women?

The answer is yes, because Jesus came to this earth and was called 'Immanuel', which means, 'God with us' (Matthew 1:23). By the way he lived his life, through his teaching and most powerfully by his death, he showed us what God is like—how much he loves us and wants us to know and depend on him. God is far beyond our limited human comprehension and yet, at the same time, he is the Father who draws near to us and takes the terror from the darkness.

## Prayer

*How good is the God we adore,*
*Our faithful unchangeable Friend!*
*His love is as great as his power*
*and knows neither measure nor end!*

JOSEPH HART (1712–68)

# Fence moving

Consequently, you are no longer foreigners and aliens, but fellow-
citizens with God's people and members of God's household.

EPHESIANS 2:19

A group of soldiers were engaged in a battle on French soil during
World War II. In a furious exchange of fire, one man was shot and
killed. When the fighting died down, the dead man's companions took
his body to a local church and asked the priest if their friend could be
buried in the cemetery.

The priest enquired if the dead soldier was a baptized Roman
Catholic. His friends replied that he was not, as he had been brought
up a Methodist. The priest offered his condolences but said the rules
clearly stated that only Catholics could be buried in the churchyard.
Yet, as a gesture of kindness, he pointed to a field next to the cemetery
and said, 'That field belongs to the church. Please bury your friend
there by the fence that marks the end of the graveyard. I am sorry but
he must be buried on the other side.'

Years later, two of the soldiers made an emotional return to the
church and searched for their friend's grave, but they couldn't find it.
They remembered digging the grave by the fence at the edge of the
cemetery, as instructed. The fence was still there, but there was no sign
of the grave and the small wooden cross they had erected.

They went across to the church and found that the same priest was
still there, although he was now an old man. They asked about their
friend's grave and listened intently as the elderly priest related his story.
'That night after you left, I could not sleep,' he told them. 'My conscience was troubled, and in the early hours I made an important
decision. Then, first thing in the morning, I went out to the graveyard

199

and moved the fence. You will find your friend's grave there inside the cemetery.'

Advent Sunday marks the beginning of the season when we remember God's gift of his Son Jesus. He didn't come to be the Saviour for one religious type, one ethnic group or one social class. Jesus didn't bother with the barriers we often build, but went out of his way to make outsiders insiders. He is the Redeemer of all who accept him.

When Jesus came, God didn't just move the fence; he took it away completely.

## For further reading

EPHESIANS 2:11–22

It is painful not to belong, to be an outsider without the rights of those 'on the inside'. But in God's family there is no need for anyone to feel an outsider, because Jesus 'has destroyed the barrier, the dividing wall of hostility' (v. 14). He has conferred the right to belong on anyone who will accept him as Saviour. Why is it, then, that in some churches the new person who comes in for the first time does not feel welcome? How sad it is when someone plucks up the courage to cross the threshold, only to feel so ill at ease that they never come back.

We may not exclude people by outright hostility but by indifference, by being so caught up with our friends that we don't even notice the newcomer. We need to remind ourselves often that we 'are being built together to become a dwelling in which God lives by his Spirit' (v. 22), and seek to notice and welcome those who are being added to God's kingdom.

## Prayer

*Lord Jesus, remind me of times when I have felt excluded and an outsider, so that I will be better at noticing others who feel that way and will know how to make them feel welcome.*

# Much-loved daughter

To those who overcome, I will give some of the hidden manna.
I will also give each of them a white stone with a new name written
on it, known only to the one who receives it.

REVELATION 2:17

Love is an amazing thing.

In a remote section of the Andes, a highland tribe attacked a lowland village, carrying off with their plunder a captured baby girl. The bandits made their way back to their mountain stronghold.

The lowlanders sent an armed group of men to counterattack and rescue the child. They travelled for some days, hot on the trail of the kidnappers, until they reached a high mountain. They couldn't scale the sheer rock walls of the mountain and, despite trying various routes to climb up and pursue their attackers, they failed.

They gave up in defeat. They were lowlanders who lacked the skill, courage and experience to tackle the high ranges. Sadly, they began preparations to break camp and return to their village.

Just at that moment, they noticed a figure climbing down the rock face, slowly and carefully. As the figure descended, they recognized it as a woman—the mother of the kidnapped baby. She had bundled the child on her back as she made her way precariously down the rock face.

When she joined them, the men greeted her and asked, with a mixture of amazement and respect, 'How did you scale that mountain when our best efforts failed?'

Smiling with relief, the mother replied, 'She wasn't your daughter.'

Luke, who wrote one of the four Gospels, uses a telling phrase to describe the transition in Jesus' life as he drew close to the events of the first Easter: 'As the time approached for him to be taken up to heaven, Jesus resolutely set out for Jerusalem' (9:51).

Jesus knew that Jerusalem meant one thing—death. Betrayal, torture, rejection and crucifixion lay ahead, yet Luke writes of him setting out with clear-sighted determination that nothing and no one would deter him from his course.

At the start of what is called Holy Week, we are reminded that the cross was not a mistake, a plan that went horribly wrong. It was a clear choice that Jesus made to bring a gift that none of us could dare dream of: freedom.

Jesus chose to walk the road that led to Jerusalem and the cross. He could see a valley of hope that lay beyond, and the millions who would find it.

Truly, love is an amazing thing.

## For further reading

LEVITICUS 15:25–31; MARK 5:25–34

The desperate woman described by Mark had suffered for twelve long years. She had had not only her physical illness to bear but also its social implications. Under Jewish law, her bleeding meant that other people had to shrink from touching anything she had touched, let alone from touching her (see Leviticus 15:26–27). She had tried everything, yet the 'care' of the doctors whose help she had sought had only caused more suffering (Mark 5:26). How lonely she must have been! She was so used to rejection that she intended to touch Jesus' cloak and slip away unnoticed. As well as a physical cure, she needed emotional healing.

Jesus recognized all the unspoken longing in her heart. When he addressed her, he called her 'Daughter', affirming her place in God's family, telling her that she belonged and was special. There are times for all of us when we have unmet needs and long to hear something comforting. How would you like Jesus to speak to you?

## Prayer

*God says to you, 'You are my much-loved child.' Thank him that he is your Father and your friend.*

# Does it hurt a lot?

*Written in March 2001*

**When Israel was a child, I loved him, and out of Egypt I called my son.**
HOSEA 11:1

The living-room sofa was packed as the mum and her three small children sat down to watch TV. The programme was a made-for-children documentary on childbirth. They sat transfixed as the film showed a woman in the final stage of labour, with the baby's head slowly emerging and the rest of its body struggling free.

Mum watched the three small viewers with interest. Suddenly the youngest spoke, his eyes not moving from the screen. 'Wow, that looks painful. Does it hurt a lot?' Mum (for whom the programme had brought back all the memories) nodded. The youngster slid back into his thoughts. Then, after a few seconds, he asked, 'And is it painful for the mummy as well?'

We tend to view circumstances through the lens of our own experience. For the mother, the focal point was the shared pain of another woman. But her child's sympathy was all with the baby.

It is a principle that works in other areas of life. For example, if you are a rambler, the closure of countryside lanes and moorland can be viewed as an inconvenience, but if you are a farmer watching neighbouring cattle herds go up in smoke because of Foot and Mouth, it's a necessary precaution. For most train travellers faced with a five-hour delay, it's an infuriating nuisance. If you have lost a loved one in a train crash, however, the delay may be a poignant reminder of the fragility of life—bringing back all kinds of grief and fear.

The tendency to evaluate things on the basis of how it affects *me* is deeply ingrained in us all. Some would view it as the survival instinct—and say that as such it should not be criticized. But at rock bottom, it is selfishness that always puts 'me' at the front of the queue.

Empathy is the ability to understand and enter into another person's feelings, and it stems from a conscious effort to get involved. In one New Testament letter, we get a glimpse of what this means. Christians are urged to care for people in need, with these words, 'Remember those in prison as if you were together with them in prison, and those who are ill-treated as if you yourselves were suffering' (Hebrews 13:3).

An old Native American proverb says, 'If you want to know how another man feels, walk a mile in his moccasins.' Or try viewing life through a different lens.

## For further reading

HOSEA 11:1–11

Being a parent can be a painful business. Watching children grow up, make the wrong choices and get hurt isn't comfortable. Sometimes things go very badly wrong. This passage in Hosea shows us our heavenly Father watching as his special people choose not to follow his ways. We hear his anguish in the words, 'But the more I called Israel, the further they went from me' (v. 2). We see his tenderness, 'It was I who taught Ephraim to walk, taking them by the arms... I lifted the yoke from their neck and bent down to feed them', and his disappointment: 'But they did not realize it was I who healed them' (vv. 3–4). Instead of abandoning the people to the consequences of their actions, however, God's 'compassion is aroused' (v. 8).

In the earthly life of Jesus, we see God getting involved and putting sinful human beings before himself: 'While we were still sinners, Christ died for us' (Romans 5:8). As his followers, we are called to put others before ourselves, to make the first move to bring healing in a fractured relationship, to meet the needs of others even when it is inconvenient or painful.

## Prayer

*Pray for any parents you know who are suffering because of their children, that they may have the resolve to keep on loving and hoping, even though it hurts a lot.*

# Hearing from God

# A surprising place for a sermon

Seated in a window was a young man named Eutychus,
who was sinking into a deep sleep as Paul talked on and on.
ACTS 20:9

Spike Milligan was a British institution. The comedian and writer made
his name through *The Goon Show* and became loved for his quirky
sideways swipes at life.

His last published words were a foreword to a book of cartoons
with a religious theme: *The Good God Guide* by John Pepper (Eagle
Publishing).

I was struck by these words from Milligan's pen, which read like an
eloquent sermon. He writes honestly about his own faith journey,
which took him from strong religious devotion in youth to non-
attendance in old age, with a fair amount of disillusionment in between.
But he confesses, 'I'm basically a Jesus man still.'

In this admission, Spike fits the profile of many people in our nation
who no longer attend church but have not abandoned their faith.
'Believing without belonging', we call it. Such people fascinate me, so I
read on to look for some hint as to why and how the rot set in.

Spike put his finger on it in one word: dullness. He found church
services mind-numbingly boring. It wasn't a case of him leaving church
so much as church leaving him. He writes:

*I remember during this period when my faith was fading that I wished
somehow, somewhere, I'd come across something humorous—a comment or
an incident—in my prayer book or Bible. One, just one line like 'And lo, Jesus
laugheth heartily' or 'Jesus sayeth "Come unto me and I will tell you a joke."'*

He continues:

*Why? Why? Why? I wonder. I suspect Christ peppered his teachings and parables with wit and repartee. He was a 'whole' man. And surely the message of religion is that we find happiness in it? As a child I had holy pictures galore, all these spiritual worthies of one sort or another, and what a dreadful po-faced lot they all were. All wrong.*

I referred to the foreword as a sermon for that is what it is, even though Spike Milligan had no intention of making it one. Real sermons are those in which God speaks in an unmistakable voice. Thankfully, when it comes to delivering them, he does not limit himself to clergy and church services.

Here was a sermon with a sharp edge and a clear point: God gave us the ability to laugh, and perhaps we should start by laughing at ourselves.

## For further reading

MATTHEW 3:1–12; ACTS 20:7–11

The sermon has a mixed reputation, depending on your experience. Some people expect to be informed and challenged by them, others to be entertained, others to be sent to sleep! When word got around that the fiery John the Baptist was preaching in the desert, people flocked to hear him. John didn't pull his punches. When he saw corruption, he spoke out. How shocking to hear the respected Sadducees and Pharisees called a 'brood of vipers' (Matthew 3:7). Who would have dared to doze off in one of John's sermons, as Eutychus did in Paul's? Anyone who has sat in an uncomfortable seat while a preacher, even a good one, has 'talked on and on' must sympathize with this young man. Fortunately his fall was not permanently fatal! His restoration to life proclaimed the power of God as eloquently as any words of Paul's could have done.

## Prayer

*Lord Jesus, I want to be awake to sermons in unexpected places. Give me a listening ear and an expectation that you will speak to me.*

# Star-gazing

*Written in August 2003*

[The Lord] took [Abram] outside and said, 'Look up at the heavens
and count the stars—if indeed you can count them.' Then he said
to him, 'So shall your offspring be.'

GENESIS 15:5

I know the weather has been the hot topic this month, but did you
know we have been on red alert for another reason throughout August?

In case you missed it, the planet Mars, the Babylonians' Star of
Death and the Romans' Harbinger of War, is closer to us this month
than it has been for the past 60,000 years.

Its distance is measured at an astonishing 34.7 million miles, and on
Wednesday it will be nearest to us at precisely 9.51 pm. Coincidentally
(or was it written in the stars?), this is National Astronomy Week and
astronomical groups around the country are opening their doors to the
public to share their fascinating hobby with a wider audience.

Mars, or the Red Planet, has intrigued star-gazers for centuries and,
in recent years, scientists have done their best to discover more about
it. But despite valiant efforts, more than half the spacecraft sent from
earth in recent years have either blown up or crashed. Only three
sets of instruments have successfully landed on Mars and, from the
information they have sent back, it doesn't seem that the planet will
become a future holiday destination.

The atmosphere on Mars is one hundred times thinner than our
own, at 95 per cent carbon dioxide, and its temperature ranges wildly
from very hot to extremely cold—in fact, colder than the Antarctic.

Another British expedition to discover more is underway. Beagle 2 was launched in June and hopes to land on Christmas Day, after a seven-month journey through space. It is hoped that this may offer more clues about life on the lonely planet.

The universe continues to fascinate, confound and puzzle us. The clear night sky reveals millions of pinpricks of light and the experts tell us that with even our most powerful instruments we cannot fully chart either the size of the universe or the number of stars within it.

In Genesis, we read of the large brush strokes of creation, with the details left tantalizingly silent. The great Creator displays his awesome power in forming the earth and the heavens, and, in one of the most astonishing statements in all literature, a casual aside is thrown in: 'He also made the stars' (Genesis 1:16).

That's a thought worth pondering as we gaze into the heavens this week.


## For further reading

GENESIS 15

This was not the first time God had spoken to Abram about his descendants (see Genesis 12:2 and 13:15), but as time had passed with no sign of an heir, Abram had apparently resigned himself to leaving his property to one of his servants (15:2). On this occasion, God directed him to look up at the stars and count them, 'if indeed you can count them'! And Abram 'believed the Lord' (v. 6).

Abram might have been content simply to know that he was going to have children and grandchildren, but God allowed him a glimpse of something much bigger: his plan for the world. Every time Abram looked up at the stars to remind himself of the promise he had believed, he was actually thinking of a promise that included you and me, Christians living all over the world right now and some still to be born. And a long time ago, many years after Abram looked up into that starry night, a single star heralded the birth of one of his descendants, Jesus, the most significant one of all.

## Prayer

*Next time you look up at the stars in the night sky, remind yourself that God, who is at work in your life, is doing something even bigger than that, and that you are a small but important part of his plan.*

# Listen carefully

*Written in October 2003*

Here I am! I stand at the door and knock. If anyone hears my
voice and opens the door, I will come in and eat with them, and
they with me.

REVELATION 3:20

In the days when telegraph was the only form of long-distance communication, Morse code operators were eagerly sought.

A company advertised one such position and, from the many
applicants, several were shortlisted for interview. They arrived at a busy,
noisy office and were told by a receptionist to complete a form and take
a seat. The group sat patiently staring at the closed office door that led
to the interview room.

After a few minutes, one of the applicants got up, walked to the
door leading to the room and walked in without knocking. The others
exchanged puzzled glances. What was he doing? He was bound to be
expelled for his impatience, they thought. But to their astonishment he
emerged a few minutes later with the man who was obviously the boss,
who announced, 'The job is taken, gentlemen. I need trouble you no
further.' The rejected applicants were furious and insisted that they at
least be given the chance to show what they could do. The whole thing
was grossly unfair, they protested.

The boss called for quiet, then explained, 'Since you arrived, the
telegraph over there has been tapping out a message. It read, "If you
can understand this, go through the door opposite and the job is
yours." This young man got the message so he gets the job.'

Last week I took part in a thanksgiving service for the work of

Children's Hospice South West. Based in Fremington near Barnstaple, it provides terminal and respite care for very sick children and offers valuable support for their families. It is a truly remarkable work undertaken by a dedicated staff team and army of volunteers. Plans are well advanced to open a second hospice near Bristol, as a result of public response to their first-class work.

The team is led by Jill Farwell, who is an energetic visionary. When I asked how she first got involved in such a vital work, she recounted how she and her husband had experienced the death of two of their own children. Having trod this lonely path, they wanted to do something to help others who were walking the same way.

Being able to hear a message above the clatter of everyday life is one thing, but to listen to God through personal pain takes something and someone quite special.

## For further reading

REVELATION 3:14–22

There are lots of obstacles that can get in the way of us hearing from God. In this passage, the lukewarm church at Laodicea is being warned about complacency, which is preventing its members from hearing God's voice. They lived in prosperous times and their material comfort kept them from seeing their spiritual neediness.

In the parable of the sower, Jesus describes the person for whom 'the worries of this life and the deceitfulness of wealth choke' the word so that it doesn't bear fruit (Matthew 13:22). Both our cares and our pleasures can distract us from being open to hearing God if we focus on them and not on him—just as the candidates for the job in the story above were able to hear the morse code but did not pay any attention to it. The message to the Laodiceans is hard but not hopeless. Jesus is very close to them, just outside the door, and he is knocking. They may have stopped listening but he has not stopped speaking. If they respond, fellowship will be restored (Revelation 3:20) and even more will be given: 'the right to sit with me on my throne' (v. 21).

# Prayer

*From the world of sin, and noise,*
*And hurry I withdraw;*
*For the small and inward voice*
*I wait with humble awe;*
*Silent am I now and still,*
*Dare not in Thy presence move;*
*To my waiting soul reveal*
*The secret of Thy love.*

CHARLES WESLEY (1707–88)

# No other name

Salvation is found in no one else, for there is no other name under
heaven given to people by which we must be saved.

ACTS 4:12

Apologies if I sound breathless, but I am just back from a working visit
to Australia and Singapore.

An experience in each country prompted some serious thinking
on the long flight home. Last weekend I was in Brisbane, where, on
Sunday, a man was awarded a doctorate by the University of Queens-
land for a thesis that set out to prove that Jesus was gay. He received a
grant of $51,000 to help with his research, which included detailed
study of astrological charts in support of his case.

Then, on Tuesday, while browsing in a bookstore in Singapore, I came
across a book entitled *What Would Jesus Eat?* It contained chapter
headings such as 'What Would Jesus Choose for Dessert?' Hoping like
crazy that it might be an elaborate wind-up, my illusions were shattered
when I realized it was a serious attempt by an American nutrition expert
to prove that the diet of a first-century Jew was healthier than a Big Mac.

Reflecting on these two incidents, I reached four conclusions. First,
that the academic world really ought to have a charge like the Football
Association does, covering things such as 'bringing the game into dis-
repute'. Second, that you can make money from anything these days—
the more bizarre the better, it seems. And third, that Jesus remains good
business even in an e-commerce world.

But the fourth conclusion is much deeper and more disturbing than
the other three. Why is Jesus the man who simply will not go away? You
can't avoid him, no matter where you travel. He even features loudly in
our profanities. As a golfer, I can't get over the number of sliced shots

217

and missed putts he is responsible for. For a poor Jewish carpenter who never travelled more than a couple of hundred miles from home, failed to write a book and handed on leadership of his movement to some very dodgy characters, he seems to have had far greater influence than should be expected.

Come to think of it, I can't think of any leader of a world religion whose name is invoked so often, which in itself offers a suggestion for a PhD that would be really useful. I've even got a title for it, from a question posed by H.G. Wells: 'Is it any wonder that to this day this Galilean is too much for our small hearts?'

## For further reading

Acts 4:1–21

The religious leaders have found, to their horror, that their attempt to suppress Jesus and the following he had built up has backfired disastrously. They have got rid of Jesus as far as they can tell, but now, instead of a small group of close followers and an easily led, sensation-seeking crowd, they are faced with about five thousand believers proclaiming that Jesus has risen. They sound completely mystified when they ask, 'By what power or what name did you do this?' Peter, who only a short while before had been too afraid to acknowledge Jesus (John 18:17), now stands boldly before them and declares that 'It is by the name of Jesus Christ of Nazareth' (Acts 4:10).

All these years later, Jesus is still the only 'name under heaven given to people by which we must be saved' (v. 12). Is it any wonder that Peter declared, 'We cannot help speaking about what we have seen and heard' (v. 20)?

## Prayer

*Thank you, Lord, for the faithfulness of Peter, John and all those through the years who have passed on the truth about who you are and what you have done, so that I, in this 21st century, can know you.*

# Windows on the World from the Word

This is a book for all of us who want to connect our everyday lives with Bible teaching—but who don't feel we have enough time to do it. Ideal for use on a daily, weekly or occasional basis, it offers 'God thoughts' on issues in today's world, showing how Christian faith can be 'earthed' in the reality of the challenges and situations that each of us, in different ways, have to face. Comments are linked to Bible passages and conclude with a prayer or thought for reflection, while a themed index helps to track down relevant teaching. And each piece is short enough to read through in ten minutes!

*ISBN 1 84101 149 5   £6.99*
*Available from your local Christian bookshop or, in case of difficulty, direct from BRF using the order form on page 223.*

# Doorways from the Word to the World

A sequel to the popular *Windows on the World from the Word*, this new book from Ian Coffey and Kim Bush once again offers an easy way into connecting Christian belief with daily life, even for those so busy that they can spare only a few minutes for reading and reflection. Taking the theme of 'doorways', we find Bible-related thoughts on issues ranging from discipleship to the Church year, taking in everything from wisdom to worship on the way.

*ISBN 1 84101 315 3   £7.99*
*Available from your local Christian bookshop or, in case of difficulty, direct from BRF using the order form on page 223.*

# Transforming the Ordinary

## Bible meditations for the everyday

## John Henstridge

This book is a series of prayer meditations based around Bible passages, which focus on helping us build awareness of God into the variety and ordinariness of our daily routines.

Fom celebrating a birthday to being stuck in a queue of traffic, the thirty meditations cover a range of familiar experiences and events, showing how we can learn, whatever our circumstances, to tune our hearts and minds into God's presence, there with us. The meditations can be used by individuals for their own personal prayer time, but the introduction also suggests ways of making use of them in a group setting.

*ISBN 1 84101 316 1   £6.99*
*Available from your local Christian bookshop or, in case of difficulty, direct from BRF using the order form on page 223.*

## ORDER FORM

| REF | TITLE | PRICE | QTY | TOTAL |
|-----|-------|-------|-----|-------|
| 149 5 | Windows on the World from the Word | £6.99 | | |
| 315 3 | Doorways from the Word to the World | £7.99 | | |
| 316 1 | Transforming the Ordinary | £6.99 | | |

| POSTAGE AND PACKING CHARGES | | | | | | |
|-----|-----|-----|-----|-----|---|---|
| Order value | UK | Europe | Surface | Air Mail | Postage and packing: | |
| £7.00 & under | £1.25 | £3.00 | £3.50 | £5.50 | Donation: | |
| £7.01–£30.00 | £2.25 | £5.50 | £6.50 | £10.00 | Total enclosed: | |
| Over £30.00 | free | prices on request | | | | |

Name _____ Account Number _____

Address _____

_____ Postcode _____

Telephone Number _____ Email _____

Payment by: ☐ Cheque ☐ Mastercard ☐ Visa ☐ Postal Order ☐ Switch

Card no. ☐☐☐☐ ☐☐☐☐ ☐☐☐☐ ☐☐☐☐

Expires ☐☐ ☐☐        Issue no. of Switch card ☐☐☐

Signature _____ Date _____

*All orders must be accompanied by the appropriate payment.*

**Please send your completed order form to:**
BRF, First Floor, Elsfield Hall, 15–17 Elsfield Way, Oxford OX2 8FG
Tel. 01865 319700 / Fax. 01865 319701  Email: enquiries@brf.org.uk

☐  Please send me further information about BRF publications.

Available from your local Christian bookshop.            BRF is a Registered Charity

# brf

## Resourcing your spiritual journey

**through...**

- Bible reading notes
- Books for Advent & Lent
- Books for Bible study and prayer
- Books to resource those working with under 11s in school, church and at home

- Quiet days and retreats
- Training for primary teachers and children's leaders
- Godly Play
- Barnabas Live

For more information, visit the **brf** website at **www.brf.org.uk**

BRF is a Registered Charity